THE SHEIK AND THE SHADOW

A Memoir of Brotherly Bond, Celebrity, and Madness

ROBERT A. BERNSTEIN

CONTENTS

Diagnosed by a Movie Star

IN 1956, MY OLDER brother Morey wrote a groundbreaking bestseller, *The Search for Bridey Murphy*, that was made into a movie starring two of the big names of the era. The *New York Times* has described the book as "one of the defining events in the popular culture of the period," and a 1988 Time-Life book, *Psychic Voyages,* stated that "Few books have seized the imagination of America as firmly as did Morey Bernstein's *The Search for Bridey Murphy* in 1956."

The book sold 6 million copies, was published in 30 languages in 34 countries, and graced the *New York Times* bestseller list for half a year. Now in its 52nd year of publication as I write, sales continue to produce annual royalties for my daughters, who inherited the copyright from their uncle.

Bridey is the story of a young Pueblo, Colorado woman who, under hypnosis by Morey—a successful local businessman who had taken up hypnotism as a hobby—spoke of what she characterized as an earlier incarnation in Ireland. In six tape-recorded trance sessions, she described in meticulous detail, and often with a thick Irish brogue, her supposed life in Cork and Belfast in the early 19th century as a lass named Bridget ("Bridey") Murphy.

The theory of reincarnation until then had been largely unknown in America, and *Bridey* spawned massive hoopla and controversy. Some critics—spurred by orthodox religious beliefs, the topic's inherent invitation to sensationalism, or both—unfairly tarred Morey as a fool, a charlatan, or worse.

Morey invited me to visit the Hollywood set, and as we toured the lot he introduced me to various people we encountered along the way. One of them was a major star of the day, Danny Kaye. Kaye shook my hand, looked at me in mock seriousness, and said, "So you're Morey's brother. Are you crazy, too?"

Morey and I laughed heartily, pleased to be the butt of a celebrity's sport. Morey ignored the implied skepticism of his work, and we both accepted the taunt in the jocular spirit in which we presumed it was intended.

But in fact, Kaye wasn't far off the mark. We were both, as our Yiddish ancestors might have put it, somewhat "meshuga": profoundly neurotic. Our respective pathologies were indelibly intertwined, forming opposite sides of the same quirky coin.

Morey would end his days dubbed by the *Denver Post* "the Howard Hughes of Pueblo"—a recluse in a tiny apartment, emaciated, with long untrimmed hair and beard, attended prior to his death in 1999 by a sole paid attendant. A local paper, the *Pueblo Chieftain*, described him as "the man who used to be this…town's most visible being and is now its most reclusive." Although a multi-millionaire, his cause of death as officially recorded on his death certificate was malnutrition.

About a year after meeting Danny Kaye, I would land in a locked ward, technically-certified as insane, at a well-known Maryland madhouse. Known as Chestnut Lodge, the institution was a sort of loony bin of last resort, famous as a last-ditch hope for cases elsewhere decreed hopeless. (It was the setting of the book, movie, and play *I Never Promised You a Rose Garden.*)

I had come to the Lodge from a Seattle mental hospital whose "discharge diagnosis" was somber but terse. It read: "Schizophrenic reaction, acute, undifferentiated type. Treatment recommendation, continued hospitalization. The prognosis is guarded."

"Guarded," I would learn, was medical-ese for "probably a lost cause."

Instead, I prospered at the Lodge—due to a patient-comes-first attitude on the part of a Lodge medical staff that a few years later would be labeled by an eminent British psychiatrist as a group of "dedicated fools." I leave to others the determination of whether their psychiatric theories were in fact foolish. But their dedication to their patients' welfare—and the good that could blossom from that dedication—is indisputable.

Some decades after my Lodge stay, I became personally friendly with Dr. Robert W. Gibson, who at the time of my admission was administrator of the locked ward to which I was committed. Later, Dr. Gibson headed Sheppard Pratt mental hospital in Baltimore for 30 years, during which he served a term as president of the American Psychiatric Association.

Bob Gibson and I spent countless hours recalling our respective experiences at the Lodge, and he made available to me extensive Lodge records of the period, including staff conference reports. It is to him that I am indebted for the material in the chapters designated "Behind the Scenes," describing my confinement there from the staff's perspective.

For me, that Maryland "crazy house" would provide perhaps the most positive experience of my life.

For Morey, *Bridey*'s worldwide fame, perversely, would speed his tragic degeneration into becoming our hometown's Howard Hughes.

So it was that our lives, though ever-intertwined, spun their diverse paths.

I

Beachhead at Normandie

MY WIFE, MYRNA, AND I routinely celebrate our wedding anniversary each year at the fashionable Normandie Farm restaurant in Potomac, Maryland, where in my eagerness to impress her I had taken her on our first date more than 40 years ago.

But for me personally, Normandie Farm also conjures some very different memories. For it was there, just a few tables away from where Myrna and I sipped our celebratory chardonnay last year, that I had dinner on my first night as a certified-insane patient at Rockville's then-famed madhouse known as Chestnut Lodge.

I HAD COME to the Lodge from Seattle's Pinel Foundation hospital, whose medical director, Dr. R. Hugh Dickinson, could hardly be blamed for the unabashed pessimism inherent in his prognosis of "guarded."

Three weeks earlier, in a suicidal spasm on a small locked ward of his 30-bed sanitarium, I had slit my wrists and throat, requiring plastic surgery to reattach the severed wrist tendons. Afterward, shaken staff members were reluctant to attend to me. Some actually refused to do so. For some 23 hours of each day, I lay in my bed beside a wall not yet wholly scrubbed clean of blood stains, forearms encased in plaster casts and shackled to the side

1

of the bed. Dickerson wrote in a report that caring for me was "exhausting the resources" of his personnel and that the staff's "undercurrent of distrust" toward me mandated my departure from Pinel.

The moment a bed became available at Chestnut Lodge, he arranged for my transfer.

The Chestnut Lodge Main Building in Rockville, Maryland / MONTGOMERY COUNTY COUNCIL

I FLEW FROM Seattle to Washington, DC, flanked by two obviously-tense psychiatric nurses. After landing in DC and taking an hour's taxi ride from National Airport, we exited the cab before a gloomily imposing, four-story 1870s brick structure in Rockville. I would come to know it as the Lodge's Main Building—the heart of an unfenced, rather bucolic, 21-acre spread that included numerous other buildings of various sizes and styles, situated along a narrow winding service road.

Inside, in a first-floor reception room, an admitting physician turned me over to an aide who said his name was Earl. Earl was a sallow, hollow-cheeked, six-foot-three string bean of a man seemingly typecast, I thought, as a sadistic

2

asylum guard. Dour and silent, he led me to a dimly-lit rear stairwell. We climbed up stone steps past the Second Floor landing, where I was startled by the face of a wild-eyed, scraggly-haired woman leering angrily through the small, square, wire-laced window of a heavy steel door. We continued up another flight to the Third Floor version of the same door, which my grim-faced escort unlocked with one of the many keys hanging from the thick ring at his waist. He swung open the door and I walked through—into what, for me, loomed as the earthly embodiment of Dante's seventh circle.

I would later learn that many of the bizarre, disheveled, drooling, groaning, pacing, gesticulating, glowering creatures before me represented some of the nation's most elite families. One was a world-famous mathematician. Another had commanded a PT boat in the Korean War. Another was the son of a man then in the news almost daily as the head of an important government agency. Another was the son of a well-known playboy notorious for a string of discarded brides that circled the globe. Still another was the brother-in-law of an ambassador. All—virtually by definition, in light of what I would discover to be the Lodge's per-day rack rate—were beneficiaries of moderate to extreme wealth.

For the moment, however, what I saw was a barren hallway peopled by characters from my most nightmarish snake-pit fantasies. Among them, against the wall to my right, a pudgy middle-aged man, dressed in ragged khakis and a torn grayish T-shirt, sat on the floor hugging his knees, rocking back and forth and muttering endlessly, "I can't shit, I can't shit." Several others simply paced, perhaps four feet one way, six the other, eyes to the floor, uttering animal-like snorts, grunts, and groans. A tall, cadaverous, seemingly-spineless figure, ghoulishly ageless, slumped against the left wall, staring vacantly into the distance. A young, solidly-built black-haired man strode purposefully toward me and thrust his face threateningly in mine. Dark eyes sparking angrily, he launched into some sort of obscenity-peppered tirade in which the Mafia seemed to figure prominently. His words, though rationally incomprehensible, were nevertheless plainly designed to evoke the fear of God—and in that, for me, he wholly succeeded, Mafia or no.

Then, standing just beyond one of the snorting pacers, I saw a strikingly attractive young woman. She wore a starched cap and white uniform that I would later recognize as the dress code of a team of student nurses from North Carolina on psychiatric training rotation. She smiled at me, and the warmth and sparkle of her brown eyes shone brightly through the bedlam around her—and kindled in me the first faint stirring of something other than dread.

The central corridor extended the length of the building, flanked by the doors to some 20 rooms. Earl guided me through a door along the left side and midway down the corridor into a room sparsely furnished with two metal frame beds, two small wooden dressers, and a pair of plywood wardrobes. Though I knew the sun to be shining outside, the room's single window, barred by heavy wire-mesh screening, shed little light. Earl told me my luggage would be brought up shortly by another aide and, pointing to the doorway behind me, said I'd be sharing this room with "Henry." I looked around to see the noodle-like frame of the emaciated humanoid I had seen in the corridor, now craning his neck through the opening, his eerily vacant stare cast generally in my direction. This, it seemed, was Henry. My roommate, I would discover, was formally diagnosed as catatonic and had not voluntarily eaten a morsel of food for some years, during which he was being tube-fed daily.

WHEN I HAD first become severely depressed in Palo Alto, California, where I was then living, I had asked a psychiatrist there to recommend a hospital that might help me. He had suggested the Lodge, but I had gone first to Pinel because the Lodge then had no available beds.

Now, terror gripped the pit of my stomach and choked the passages of my throat, and I thought, dear God, what have I done? In their most fevered imagination, could a Dickens or a Poe have envisioned a more bone-chilling plight?

Earl departed, and in his wake entered a thirty-something, business-like woman dressed in a blue woolen skirt and gray-checked cotton blouse. She introduced herself as Gloria George, the charge nurse, and asked me to follow her into the nursing station—a cramped cubicle behind a Dutch door adjacent to my (and Henry's) bedroom. There, she unwrapped the ace bandages that held my half-casts in place, examined and dressed the wounds and rewrapped the casts. She asked a few questions regarding vital statistics and entered the answers on some sort of official form. She said someone she identified only as Brian would be bringing my luggage to the room, and then added with, to me, shocking casualness: "I hope you packed some dress clothes. Your brother and sister-in-law want to have dinner at a restaurant where you'll need a coat and tie."

This was the first I knew that my brother, Morey, and his wife, Hazel, then living in New York, had come to Rockville for my arrival. More stunningly—after three weeks of dungeon-like restraint followed by today's Kafkaesque events—her words seemed to drift in from some outer world. The thought of dining at a fashionable restaurant, and with members of my own family, actually struck me as eerie and frightening. Over the past weeks, the "real world" had become, for me, quite unreal and deeply scary.

A tall broad-shouldered young man with curly dark hair appeared at the door, greeted Gloria, and informed me, smiling, that my baggage was in my room. Gloria told me this was Brian and that he would be "specialing" me through the evening and until 6 a.m. "Special," it seemed, was the Lodge euphemism for one-on-one sentry duty. I would be "specialed"—accompanied by an aide 24 hours a day, eating, sleeping, going to the bathroom—for some two weeks, until the staff finally became convinced that I intended no physical harm to myself or others.

So it was that a few hours later—dressed in an untidy blue blazer, shirt, and tie, all badly crumpled from weeks in a cramped suitcase—I found myself part of a rather odd foursome at Normandie Farm, a few miles west of Rockville. For my part, I sat, brain spinning, unable to reconcile the sumptuous ambience and polite dinner-talk with the bizarre, frightening surroundings to which I knew I would soon be returning. Brian, Morey, and Hazel engaged in somewhat strained chitchat, relative strangers caught in a kind of unnatural intimacy. I sat in virtual silence, my mind stubbornly returning to visions of Henry. Was my wraith-like roommate, I wondered, an apparition of my own destiny? For now, bereft of whatever minor conversational graces I might have once possessed, I was grateful for Brian's presence.

His obviously genuine interest in the celebrity status of my brother—then enjoying worldwide fame as the author of a bestseller recently made into a movie—eased the conversational tension. My terror of the afternoon did not fade. Still, as I half-listened to the casual table talk, I experienced something I hadn't felt for months: a spark of hope.

The warm smile of a brown-eyed student nurse… the matter-of-fact treatment by a charge nurse who seemed to regard me not merely as deranged patient but also as functioning human being… the companionship, however mutually-involuntary, of a friendly young man named Brian… reunion with family members in an elegant countryside eatery…

A few hours later, back at the Lodge, Henry made his move to douse, rather literally, any incipient gleam of hope. Lying abed on my side in the dark, with Brian nodding and fighting to stay awake in a chair at the foot of the bed, I turned onto my back to find Henry standing above me, penis dangling over my head, ready to urinate. I screamed, and Brian leapt to a nick-of-time rescue.

I had not heard Henry speak a word—few at the Lodge ever had. But he was plainly capable of conveying, quite articulately, how he felt about a stranger usurping his privacy.

II

The Sheik and the Shadow

MY BROTHER MOREY AND I grew up in Pueblo, Colorado, then a rather grimy steel town along the Rockies' Front Range, where our Russian immigrant grandfather and his brother founded a business begun as a junkyard in 1890. My father and uncle took over on his death in 1917, and Morey, nearly seven years my senior, added various farm and construction equipment lines after completing college in 1941. The Pueblo Convention Center is located on the former site of the business, and one of its meeting sites is named the Bernstein Brothers Room.

I think of our father and mother now with affection and sadness. They were well-meaning, good, and decent people—but wildly mismatched, constantly at odds, emotionally insecure, and basically unfit for parenting.

Dad spent long hours at work and his insecurity showed up in obsessive fault-finding with others. Once, for example, when Morey ordered a boxcar of barbed wire, Dad angrily criticized him, predicting, "You won't sell that for 10 years!" When in fact the wire sold rather speedily, his complaint became, "Why did you only order one carload?"

Morey and Bob with their father Sam, in a photo displayed at the Pueblo Convention Center

Other than to contemplate the day when I would join him in the business, he paid no discernible attention to my upbringing—concerned in the meantime, so far as I could tell, only that I not bother him. Once, when I was 11, I arrived home from school on a spring afternoon to find him waiting for me in the living room. He told me that Morey had been in an accident and was in the hospital and that my mother was there with him. I broke into tears—at which he cuffed the side of my head with sufficient force to knock me to the floor. My display of emotion, apparently, was too much for him to abide.

Our mother was essentially kind and sweet-natured but also ever-anxious and high-strung. She treated me with a kind of mother-hen nervousness that in both manner and words conveyed to me that I was abnormally sensitive and "sickly." She told me to remember that I was "not as strong as the other boys." In both my third and fourth grades, she obtained permission from the school to allow me to stay home and nap during the afternoon sessions of school. As far as she was concerned, if I tired of a yard work job, no problem: I could just stop and go in the house. I even recall occasions on which she hired a good friend of mine to mow, rake, and dig dandelions while I watched or sat in the house reading.

Although I enjoyed playing sports with my friends and later lettered in high school basketball, I never openly challenged her assessment of my weakness. And later, even when I ranked third in strength and endurance in my Navy boot camp company of 150 men, my self-perception remained essentially unchanged.

IN A CHILDHOOD HOME that for me felt bleak and cold and unexciting, Morey provided the sole ray of light and hope. He was my idol and role model. We called each other "chum"—he was "big chum," I was "little chum"—and I reveled in the implied intimacy of the terms. He was a scholar and an athlete, handsome, brilliant, an apparent winner at everything he tried. He was my mentor in all respects. He taught me how to study, to appreciate literature and a good joke, how to box, field a grounder, and shoot a basket, how to handle myself on my first date. He took me fishing and showed me how to build a crystal set in a cigar box that, with earphones, would actually bring in the local radio station.

The driving imperative of my life was to pattern my being after my adored big brother. Inevitably I would fall short. Into adulthood, my consolation was to bask in the aura of his reflected glory—unaware of the extent to which my adoration was a reflection of the void at my core.

From boyhood, Morey seemed to have it all—brains, looks, grace, talent, charm. As a young man, he resembled a blond Frank Sinatra (though better-looking), and at college in Philadelphia he claimed to have been mobbed, mistaken for the crooner, by crazed bobbysoxers. He retained his boyish handsomeness and slim, broad-shouldered athlete's body through middle age. His striking good looks, complemented by a quick and penetrating wit and ever-restless curiosity, generated a kind of magnetism that made him a natural focus of attention.

As a teenager, his friends nicknamed him "Sheik," after the signature role of then film heartthrob Rudolph Valentino. The most popular girls competed for his favors. "All the girls found him attractive—a pretty boy with his blond curly hair and big gray eyes," recalled high school classmate Edna Falk, when I spoke with her shortly after Morey's death in 1999. Edna admitted to having then been "smitten" with him. "He was such a cute thing... and very clever and funny." But he "went after the real cute, sort of unattainable girls" and had a reputation as sort of a "rake," she said.

Throughout high school, Morey never received less than an A. To my mind, the final proof that he was the best at anything he tried came when he was 15 and won out over scores of competitors for the exotic job of spinning yo-yos in floor demonstrations at a local department store. His classmates elected him head cheerleader in both his junior and senior years. He starred in the lead role of the senior play. He was the varsity basketball team's top defensive player. I was dismayed when he placed only third in the high school popularity contest. And when he left to attend college "back East," I cried secretly in my bed at night. I rejoiced when he graduated and returned home to join our father and uncle in the family business.

An honors graduate of the Wharton School of Finance at the University of Pennsylvania, he slipped easily into the role of take-charge businessman. He expanded the firm in numerous new directions, including one fencing product based on his own patented design. As a savvy investor, he solidified the family financial well-being and became friendly with some of the nation's leading securities market gurus. One personal friend, for example, was the late Benjamin Graham, whom financial guru Warren Buffett has described as being the second most important man in Buffett's life, after only his father.

At 28, Morey married Hazel Higgins, a cosmetician and statuesque blonde of warmth, intelligence, and natural beauty who had no need of her own professional skills.

Then, in his mid-thirties he parlayed his parlor-hypnotism hobby into the controversial *Bridey* bestseller. The *Denver Post* wrote of him, "If not [Pueblo's] wealthiest man—he's certainly on the list—he goes unchallenged as its most interesting."

Morey

So morey was the family megastar. I was the also-ran, even something of a clan pariah. Hopelessly-unsure of myself in a business setting, I shuddered inwardly at the assumption that I would of course join Morey, my father, and my uncle in the family enterprise. But tellingly, it was only via my first mental breakdown, complete with suicide attempt and hospitalization, that I managed to convey that distaste—and to elicit the reluctant support of Morey and the others for what they privately considered my base disloyalty.

Like so many others, I failed to spot the danger signs in Morey's luminous personality: the intensity of his insatiable ambition and the pervasive insecurity that impelled him to avoid situations in which he was not command central, surrounded by those who, like me, looked to him unquestioningly for guidance, direction, and approval.

Despite my pervasive inner sense of inadequacy, my outward appearance up to about age 25 included some of the trappings of a model middle-class youth of the era. In high school I made top grades, lettered in varsity basketball, and dated some of the more popular girls. I graduated during World War II, served two years in the Navy, and was discharged a petty officer third class. After the war, I graduated from Stanford University, where I qualified for the engineering scholastic honor society and served as sports editor of the campus daily and briefly as president of my fraternity.

Beneath this veneer of normalcy, however, seethed a cauldron of anxiety. I was convinced that at root I was worthless, and maybe crazy. If people complimented me, I secretly thought them either flatterers or too easily duped. When, like Morey, I finished high school with straight As, I told myself I had really learned nothing—that the grades simply reflected a meaningless talent for test taking.

I was ecstatic to be elected president of my college fraternity—but soon resigned in terror of botching the job the first time a genuine controversy arose among the brothers. I preened when told I was being considered as the next editor of the college newspaper—but then panicked and found an excuse to withdraw my name from consideration.

Though compelled to strain for triumphs in the mode of my brother, I experienced every success as tenuous—part of a false facade masking the reality of some hazily-defined but awesome inner defect. Scariest of all, I never recall being wholly free of the fear of insanity, with the ugly brown brick buildings of the nearby Colorado State Hospital looming as some omnipresent omen. At an early age, going there with Morey to visit a friend of his whose father was a hospital employee, I saw something that etched itself indelibly in my memory: the image of three wild-eyed, wild-haired women screaming at us while scratching madly at the screen that contained them inside a cantilevered walkway between two buildings.

I was convinced that being more like Morey—smart, strong, capable, clever, glamorous, successful—represented the only escape from the agonies that haunted me. Life became an endless effort to behave in ways designed to convince myself and others that I too possessed the traits I so admired in him.

It was a balancing act that absorbed massive amounts of psychic energy. It was perhaps inevitable that I would ultimately be overwhelmed by the pent-up horrors.

Bob

14

Bob and Morey

III

Behind the Scenes: A Prescription of Hope

As chestnut lodge's third-floor administrator, Dr. Robert W. Gibson had received dire warnings from Pinel that the staff there had found me simply too much to handle. Advance billing pictured me as psychotic, suicidal, and, at least where my self-destructive intentions were concerned, wholly untrustworthy.

In Pinel's report to the Lodge, Dr. Dickinson wrote, "Even though we have a very high ratio of ward personnel to patients… the nature of his agitation was such as to keep the experienced ward personnel constantly in doubt." A second Pinel doctor stressed the absolute requirement that I be placed in "maximum security."

Thus, Dr. Gibson felt he had no choice but to special me around the clock and firm up the ward's suicide precautions generally. But Dr. Gibson had other priorities as well. He was convinced that a patient's first 24 hours at the hospital could be critical—as important, he felt, as the entire first six months—to the ultimate outcome of treatment: a certain amount of risk, inherent in dispatching a new patient with a gory résumé to an upscale French restaurant for his first meal in Gibson's custody, was not wholly antithetical to Lodge routine.

Suicide precautions at basically every other mental institution of the time dictated removing a depressed patient's shoelaces and belt as possible devices of strangulation. But Gibson balked at this, too, in deference to his memory of a staff lecture given at the Lodge by Thomas Main, a leading British psychiatrist:

In a charade of a patient shorn of shoelaces and belt, Dr. Main shuffled painstakingly around the podium, both hands clutching his waistband to hold up his pants, as he grumbled, "By God, if I had to spend my life like this, I'd want to kill myself, too!"

So it was that I retained my laces and belt.

A tape recording of a Third Floor conference shortly before my arrival reveals their concern for both ward safety and my long-range welfare:

DR. GIBSON: "It's possible to think so much about the suicide threat that we don't think much about the person."

CHARGE NURSE GLORIA GEORGE: "It's a pity we have to disturb the entire ward for one new patient."

GIBSON: "That's true. But it wouldn't be good for him to know he's inconveniencing everybody. We need to do it in a low-key way."

AIDE: "Won't he appreciate being kept from killing himself?"

GIBSON: "This guy evidently feels he doesn't deserve to be on the face of the earth anyway. Knowing that a dozen people are suffering because of him won't be the happiest way to come into a new place. It could just reinforce his low self-esteem."

AIDE: "Are we going to take away his glasses? He *did* use them to hurt himself."

GIBSON: "Only at night when he's sleeping."

Twenty-four-hour Specials would provide most of the needed protection, he decided, and Nurse George had already lined up some of the more trusted aides to handle that duty. Dr. Gibson left for later the knottier questions of when and how to safely relax the one-on-one guard.

He suspected that what happened at Pinel demonstrated a rather sinister cycle of interaction that can develop when a patient's mood of hopelessness infects staff members—who then convey a tacit message of "You're hopeless, and we're helpless."

To break that emotional logjam, Gibson wanted to make clear to me that "things are going to be different from now on." So it was that he decided to use the presence of Morey and Hazel, who had arrived without notice three days earlier.

Dr. Robert Gibson

He asked the aide Earl Butt, whose judgment he trusted, if Earl foresaw any problems with my going to dinner with Morey and Hazel so long as I was accompanied by a Special. Earl said he did not, but that he was busy that evening. So Dr. Gibson decided that Brian—husky, strong, and easygoing—could fill in as Special, and the Normandie outing was set.

Because of the fame of his book, Morey had created a stir at the Lodge when he arrived three days before. Many of the more functional patients crowded around to speak with the then-celebrity author and ask questions about Bridey. Morey and Hazel even attended a cocktail hour held weekly at the "open" Hilltop residence, which housed patients not confined to a locked ward.

Taking advantage of their presence, clinical administrator Clarence Shulz interviewed Morey and Hazel separately and asked a Lodge social worker to do likewise.

Shulz and the social worker both concluded that Morey had substantial personal problems that were deeply intertwined with mine. The social worker's report saw in him a quality of "goodness," but at the same time she described him as "extremely hostile," "highly suspicious," and "extremely controlling." And, she reported, Hazel "expressed great fear that Morey was ready to crack up, and was perhaps sicker than Bob."

For Dr. Gibson, nevertheless, Morey's arrival presented an opportunity to help deliver that message that "things are going to be different" at the Lodge.

But once the Normandie dinner had accomplished its purpose of conveying the message, neither Dr. Gibson nor Dr. Schulz wanted Morey around. The next day, Dr. Schulz told Morey that I would not be allowed any visitors during an indefinite adjustment period. The staff shed no tears when Morey and Hazel left for New York, where they were then living.

DR. SCHULZ AND THE SOCIAL WORKER had both been put off by Morey's obvious willingness to relieve the Lodge staff of the responsibility for designing my treatment plan. The social worker reported that Morey "was really quite frantic when he learned that we were not going to give Bob shock treatment."

At Pinel, Morey had in fact significantly affected my treatment plan, and among other things had successfully pressed the staff—contrary to its usual policy—to give me electric shock. Some years later, on a visit to Seattle, I would speak with two of the doctors at Pinel—and however foggy their memories might otherwise be of a long-ago case, they would nevertheless vividly recall Morey's vigorous pressures. (Morey's interference is actually a matter of public record: A subsequent study of the Pinel operation (*End of Hope*, 1988) concluded that Morey had created an ongoing problem and significantly influenced my treatment there.)

The social worker's written report, and her comments at a staff conference some days later, reflect how she saw the general outlines of my relationship with Morey: She said I had looked to Morey more as father than sibling from the time I was very young, and that he in turn acted much like "a guilty parent." His attitude of "fierce protectiveness," she thought, was accompanied by a sharp resentment at my failure to join him in either the Pueblo business or his subsequent New York investment activity. She said he felt as though he had been forced to "take all the hard knocks for Bob with the family."

In all, she did not paint a pretty picture of Morey. While she saw him as a person of apparent "goodness" and "very good intelligence," she sensed a restless aggression and driving needs to prove himself and to exercise "perfect control." (She presumably would have nodded "amen" to a roughly contemporary description of Morey by a Pueblo newspaperman: "He has a vast amount of physical energy and mental agility that at times makes him appear as a restless animal, worrying his mind also is caged and at times unable to penetrate subjects to which he applies it.")

The social worker described Morey's passion for making money ("He told me in any number of different ways that that is the only thing which is important"), but noted that he was at the same time "pursuing parapsychology with a zealous passion" as though "trying to make a tremendous name for himself in this field."

From her conversation with Hazel, she learned that Hazel and Morey were unable to have children, and that in general—due largely to Morey's almost total absorption with parapsychology and investment interests—Hazel felt she "had no roots in the marriage."

Presumably, the social worker would not have been surprised by the significant events to come in Morey's life: his continued restless ambition in both mainstream finance and the offbeat world of psychics and clairvoyants, his unhappy divorce, and his final years of eccentric Howard Hughes-like isolation.

EARLY ON, Lodge doctors saw a connection between my disorder and my brother's fascination with hypnosis.

In a memorandum summarizing early reports he had received from other doctors, the director of psychiatry would observe that in my relationship with Morey, I "behaved like a hypnotic subject who is fearful of being controlled and yet invites just that kind of control."

Dr. Gibson later told me that he had taken a certain professional interest in hypnosis as a psychiatric tool. Early in his career, he had found the "age-regression" technique—transporting a subject to their state of mind at any given age—to be potentially useful. But, he said, "I had abandoned hypnosis, quite frankly, because of the uneasiness associated with what to me felt a little too much like playing God." When I arrived on his ward, he had wondered to what extent my problems might turn on the fact that my "hypnotist brother had assumed that very kind of God-like role toward an initially willing, even eager, little brother." It was a view reinforced by Dr. Jackson's report from Palo Alto, stating that I had early in life adopted a "magic cloak of helplessness" as a hoped-for protective coat of psychic armor.

So while he had personally forsaken hypnotism as a therapeutic tool, Dr. Gibson nevertheless seemed to have inherited responsibility for a hypnotically-entranced subject—a sort of harbinger to Bridey Murphy.

IV

"Something For Freaks, Isn't It?"

TWO OF MOREY'S HIGH school friends would have seconded the Lodge social worker's observations as to Morey's quality of "goodness" and the strong element of self-centeredness in his personality.

Shortly after Morey's death, his friend Herb Elliott told me that Morey had "a fantastic influence" on his life. Elliott described himself as a "shy, retiring guy with a kind of deep inferiority complex" until Morey helped him to "come out of my shell and assume a leadership role" in high school: "Morey set standards for me that I otherwise never would have thought I could have achieved." Elliott sobbed as he recalled writing Morey a letter shortly before he died: "I told him how much I loved him and how much he had influenced my life."

Elliott and classmate Edna Falk nevertheless would second the social worker's observation that Morey's personality included a strong element of self-centeredness and a quality that today might merit him the label of control freak. "Let's face it," Elliott told me, "he was an egomaniac—but in a nice kind of way." (Morey might even have agreed: One of his favorite quips was, "One of my countless virtues is my modesty.")

Falk would personally witness the deterioration in Morey that followed the enormous *Bridey* success. As an actress living in New York in the 1950s under the stage name Katherine Gregg, Edna was close to Morey and Hazel in "the Bridey years." During the book's preparation, she typed the original transcripts of the six "Bridey" hypnotic sessions and later assisted in the gargantuan task of responding to the voluminous flow of reader mail.

She saw first-hand both Morey's rise to stardom and his subsequent retreat into isolation.

NEARLY A HALF-CENTURY LATER, a retired Pueblo banker recalled for me nearly every detail of the spring night in 1952 when he introduced Morey to Virginia "Ginny" Tighe, the woman destined to be known to the world as Bridey Murphy. And some months after that fateful meeting, the banker would become one of five persons to witness a hypnotized Ginny launch the eerie tale that would captivate the nation and the world.

Morey's friendship with that banker, "Tink" Snapp, ultimately spanned more than seven decades. They grew up a few blocks apart on Pueblo's North Side, and I remember as a little boy being captivated by what to me was their astonishing athletic prowess, watching them go one-on-one at a neighbor's backyard iron hoop. Both were starters on the Centennial High School basketball varsity. Tink describes the innate athletic grace that allowed Morey as a raw tennis novice at 15 to outplay virtually all his more experienced competitors. He chuckles in memory of Morey's writing, acting, and comedy skills as co-producer of weekly "pep assembly" skits.

Later, Tink was a vice president of the Pueblo bank where Morey served a four-year stretch as a director. Eventually, during Morey's reclusive final years, Tink was one of the few friends with whom Morey kept in even sporadic telephone contact.

Both were members of Pueblo's Minnequa Club on the night in 1952 when Morey met Ginny Tighe. Morey and Hazel had joined Tink and his wife, Jane, at the Club, with five other couples. One couple was new to Morey and Hazel: Hugh Tighe, a local businessman, and his pretty, green-eyed wife, Ginny. Tink and Morey got to talking, and Tink asked if Morey had been doing anything interesting other than making money. Tink recalls:

"He said he'd been experimenting with hypnotism. So I asked, 'That's something for freaks, isn't it, Morey?' And he said something like, 'Well then, you're looking at a freak.'"

Virginia "Ginny" Tighe (aka Ruth Simmons)

MOREY HAD BY THEN become deeply entranced by various aspects of paranormal psychological phenomena, including extrasensory perception, mental telepathy, clairvoyance, and reincarnation. He knew better than to spring all this *outré* stuff on the Snapps and their friends all at once. But always eager to display his newfound talents, he invited the entire group to the Bernstein home on Logan Street, not far from the Club, for a simple demonstration of hypnosis.

An hour later, with the living-room lights dimmed, everyone sitting in a loose circle, Morey lit a candle and directed the others to focus on the flame's bright core. That flame, he told them, would become a symbol of sleep—and that as he talked to them, they would become sleepier and sleepier. Then, he said, he would count to three, and they would drift into a pleasant sleep.

"There must have been 12 or 14 of us," Tink remembered. "Nothing at all happened to me, but almost immediately I saw Barbara Cartwright's head droop, then Ginny's, then some of the others. At first, I thought they were faking, and I almost joked about it out loud. Then I realized something actually seemed to be happening."

Morey told the others that they would return to full consciousness when he counted down from ten to one, and that they'd feel very relaxed and healthy. Afterward, some of them said that's exactly how they felt—they seemed delighted with the experience. Both Barbara and Ginny, moreover, remembered absolutely nothing of the hypnotic trance. Morey said that indicated they were the best possible subjects: the so-called "somnambulist" type.

Some weeks later Morey called Tink to tell him Ginny had agreed to undergo age regression, and invited him and Jane to witness a session. They agreed, and sat rapt as Ginny recounted childhood happenings at various ages in minute detail. Tink remembers in particular that, at Morey's suggestion, Ginny wrote her name with a quick flourish while regressed to age 18—but that when he guided her back to age four, she could no longer write, only print in a childish scrawl.

Morey and Ginny

Then on November 29, 1952, the Snapps sat in on what would become the most famous of Ginny's hypnotic sessions in the Bernstein living room. It was preserved that night on a massive (then-state-of-the-art) reel-to-reel tape recorder using seven-inch spools. But the Snapps were unaware that, with the approval of Ginny and Hugh, Morey intended to try something different that evening.

Tink was emotionally unprepared for the eerie scene that followed.

"I was so confused at first, I couldn't understand what was happening," he said.

V

"Why Did They Name You 'Friday'?"

First, Morey took Ginny back to a time in her native Chicago when she was seven, and then five, eliciting various matters about her schooling, friends, toys, and a favorite black dress. Then he took her to age three (she spoke of a "little colored doll" with a dirty diaper) and on to age one ("What do you say when you want a drink of water?" "Wa-wa." "What do you say when you want a glass of milk?" "Uh… can't say that"). Finally, Morey made the big leap, taking Ginny "over the hump" and into an apparent past life. From the tape:

> MOREY: "I want you to keep on going back and back and back in your
> mind. And, surprising as it may seem, strange as it may seem,
> you will find that there are other scenes in your memory.
> There are other scenes from faraway lands and distance places
> in your memory. I will talk to you again. I will talk to you again
> in a little while… Meanwhile, your mind will be going back,
> back, back, and back until it picks up a scene—until, oddly
> enough, you will find yourself in some other scene, in some
> other place, in some other time—and when I talk to you again
> you will tell me about it. You will be able to talk to me about it
> and answer my questions. And now, just rest and relax while
> these scenes come into your mind. [Pause.] Now you're going

to tell me, now you're going to tell me what scenes came into your mind. What did you see? What did you see?"

GINNY (in the voice of a little child and a faint brogue that grows thicker as the tape proceeds): "Uh... scratched the paint off all my bed. Jus' painted it 'n made it pretty. It was a metal bed, and I scratched the paint off of it. Dug my nails on every post and just ruined it. Was jus' terrible."

—"Why did you do that?"

—"Don't know. I was just mad. Got an awful spanking."

—"What is your name?"

—"Uh, Friday."

To Morey and most of the listeners, it sounded as though she had said "Friday." In asking the next question, Morey's tone showed obvious confusion:

MOREY: "Don't you have any other name?"

GINNY: "Uh... Friday Murphy."

—"And where do you live?"

—"I live in Cork... Cork."

—"And what is the name of your mother?"

—"Kathleen."

—"And what is the name of your father?"

—"Duncan... Duncan... Murphy."

—"How old are you?"

—"Uh... four... four years old."

—"And you scratched the paint off your metal bed?"

—"Yes... scratched the paint off."

—"All right. Now see if you can see yourself a little older. See if you can see yourself when you're five, or six, or seven, or see yourself when you're an older girl. Are you a girl or a boy?"

—(rather testily) "A girl."

A series of further question elicited that her brother's name was Duncan, that she lived in a two-story wooden house in Ireland, that another brother had died as an infant when she was four, that her father was a "barrister… downtown." Then Morey asked a question that triggered obvious annoyance:

MOREY: "Why did they name you Friday?"

GINNY: (impatiently) "Bridey… Bridey."

—"Oh, I see, Bridey. Why did they name you that?"

—"Named me after my grandmother, Bridget… 'n I'm Bridey."

Further questioning evoked a sketch of the various stages of Bridey's life. She talked about her family members; about her attendance at a Mrs. Strayne's Day School (where she learned "house things" and "proper things"); about her marriage to Brian MacCarthy; about moving with Brian to Belfast, where he was attending school; about their subsequent life in Belfast after Brian became a barrister; in sadness, about the fact they had no children. She said that although she had been raised Protestant, Brian was Catholic, and in Belfast she attended St. Theresa's Catholic Church, where the priest was Father John Goran. She even discussed her own death at 66, after she "fell down on the stairs… broke some bones in my hip" and then "just sort of… withered away." Death came on a Sunday, she said, while "Brian was to church."

A scene from "The Search for Bridey Murphy" (1956)

WITH VARIOUS FRIENDS of the Bernsteins and Tighes as observers, there would be five more sessions. Under trance, "Bridey" would provide a legion of intricate details about her life in Ireland. A few years later, *Life* magazine would describe her account as containing a "wealth of subtle and plausible Irish detail [strewn] generously and casually through her long recitations." Another magazine, *Top Secret,* would write: "What made her story chillingly persuasive was the mass of circumstantial detail about people, places and customs that Mrs. Tighe recovered, although she could have known nothing about them in her waking life." Thirty-five years later, a Time-Life book would call Ginny "the all-time superstar among past-life subjects." Tink Snapp, present at one of the later five sessions, has an especially vivid memory of Ginny, normally an indifferent dancer, performing a sprightly Irish jig. She used words like "barrister," "tuppence," and "foodstuffs" that were alien to her everyday vocabulary but common in 19th-century Ireland. She correctly described the ruins of Dunluce Castle on the shore of County Antrim. She referred to the names of forgotten 19th-century Irish newspapers, schools, obscure Belfast stores, the Irish hero Cú Chulainn, and the legends of Deirdre, about which (as Ginny Tighe) she was consciously totally unaware.

Ginny herself was astounded when she listened to the tape. She didn't believe in reincarnation and couldn't imagine where "Bridey's" information came from. Ginny had never even been abroad, much less to Ireland, and she said that the only contact she remembered with anything remotely Irish was watching a stage production of the musical *Brigadoon.* (In fact, *Brigadoon* was about a Scottish village and had nothing to do with Ireland). She was amazed—though also, in a sense, bored: "My own life is much more interesting. Bridey is dull."

Without exception, regardless of their prior beliefs or religious convictions, all the witnesses came away convinced that some paranormal influence played a role in Ginny's account under hypnosis. Decades later, many of them would tell me of their persuasion. Tink Snapp was one of them. Another was Joseph Bullen, retired president and board chairman of Fountain Sand & Gravel Co. of Pueblo. Still another was Morey's ex-wife, Hazel, who generally had little else of a positive nature to say about the man she loved but could not live with, and from whom she would be divorced (quite non-amicably) 10 years after the initial "Bridey" session.

Although he had heard of similar results by other hypnotists, Morey was at first as surprised by Ginny's responsiveness as Tink or anyone else. But by the end of the third session in January 1953, he had already written a few chapters of a proposed book and was seeking ways of spreading the news to the public at large.

He contacted an editor of the local Pueblo newspaper, who said he wouldn't sully his pages with such obvious hokum. Bill Barker, a writer for the *Denver Post*'s Sunday magazine, *Empire,* reacted similarly when he first heard about the phenomenon from his brother-in-law Robert Gast, a prominent Pueblo attorney.

"The thing sounded like some sort of hoax," Barker would later write. He soon changed his mind after hearing all six tapes—interviewing the participants and observers, and watching his own wife Lydia under hypnosis by Morey prattle convincingly of an earlier lifetime. Lydia described a scene in which as a young girl she stood in the summertime heat beside a country road amid green meadows and leafy oak trees, watching soldiers march past carrying a flag with "stars in a circle." That of course is a description of the flag adopted by the Continental Congress used between 1777 and 1795.

Barker decided that the "Bridey" experiment was at least newsworthy. The result was a major three-part series by Barker in *Empire,* titled "The Strange Search for Bridey Murphy." It excited more reaction than anything the magazine had published previously—inspiring more than 10,000 letters from readers—and hinted at what was to come.

By the time the *Empire* series appeared in 1954, Morey had made his break from the Pueblo business operation. He and Hazel rented an apartment in New York at 7th Avenue and 16th Street, where he could continue work on the book while studying investments under the renowned stock market analyst Benjamin Graham. His investment classes at Columbia led to a close friendship with Graham, whose classic studies have remained standard business school fare. Meanwhile, through a mutual friend, he had met the principal of a New York publishing house which was interested in the project but ultimately rejected it as "too controversial." A second major publisher felt the same way but introduced Morey to an editor at Doubleday & Co., which agreed to a contract. By late 1955, Morey had finished the book.

A portion of the Bernstein display / PUEBLO CONVENTION CENTER

Doubleday optimistically ordered a print run of 10,000 copies, and after closing hours on January 5, 1956, prepared a double-window display of several hundred copies at its flagship Broadway store. That night, Morey and Hazel huddled together at the storefront in the Manhattan cold, awed by the merchandising mosaic and wondering what the morrow would bring.

What happened, as Hazel put it, is that "things just went crazy."

VI

"Doin' The 'Bridey Murphy Rock and Roll'"

THAT BROADWAY WINDOW DISPLAY quickly dissolved, as a stampede of buyers drained the store's entire supply of copies. In Chicago, it happened with a single stroke when a man walked into a bookstore there with a *Bridey* window display and said, "I'll take it"—buying all 166 copies to give to friends. Sales soared nationwide. A 12-inch, 33-rpm record of Ginny's original November 19, 1952 session rapidly sold 30,000 copies at a price close to that of the book itself.

In the popular mind, said *Tomorrow* magazine, the Bridey Murphy craze threatened to rival "the tulip mania of the 17th century and expressions of mass hysteria." *Time* magazine said it "made reincarnation a fad more entrancing than…flying saucers." *Writers Newsletter* declared that it "has more interest, more hold on the reader than much of the science fiction or detective plots today." The *New York Times* would later recall that "it created a cultural brush fire, elevating hypnotism into something of a national mania…"

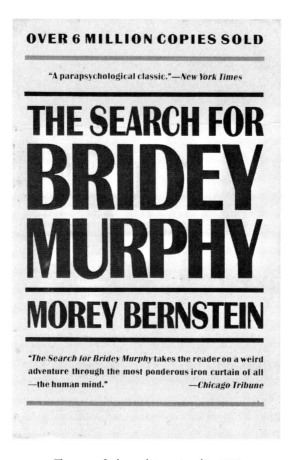

The cover of a later edition printed in 1989

Bridey rode the *Times* bestseller lists for 26 weeks, and the early reviews were mostly raves. The *Times* called it "a parapsychological classic" and "a charming book." "There are several things you can do about Bridey… but there is one thing you cannot do: put it down after you have started reading it," said the *Pittsburgh Press*. *Life Magazine* predicted, "There are few who can go through its pages without being shaken or impressed." *Newsday* called it "a tantalizing mystery story…that will provoke and stimulate the reading." Verdicts of "spellbinding," "provocative," and "stimulating" peppered the reviews.

To protect Ginny, the book had identified her by the pseudonym Ruth Simmons. But she began receiving letters addressed only to "Bridey Murphy,

Pueblo, Colorado." And when a *Time* magazine story printed her real name and address, she was inundated with telephone calls, a big bundle of daily mail, and a steady parade of people pointing at her house from the windows of passing cars. Intensely uncomfortable at the furor, she turned down a $15,000 offer (nearly $200,000 in today's dollars) for a single week's appearance at a nightclub. Within the next year, she would pass up similar offers totaling some $250,000 in 1956 dollars. She declined, for example, to recreate her sessions under hypnosis on TV's *Colgate Comedy Hour*. She had her telephone number changed 13 times in three months. She later told a reporter, "If I had known what was going to happen, I would never had lay down on that couch."

Interest in both hypnotism and reincarnation mushroomed. Newspapers teemed with ads offering to teach hypnotism. A correspondence course on hypnotism sold 250,000 copies. A hypnotist offered "to establish the prior existence of all comers" at $25 per existence. A craze of "come as you were" costume parties broke out throughout the country. Restaurants offered "reincarnation cocktails."

Television comics had a field day with *Bridey* one-liners: "Did you hear about the man who read Bridey Murphy and changed his will to leave everything to himself?" "Parents are greeting newborns with, 'Welcome back.'"

Bridey prompted at least three popular songs: "The Ballad of Bridey Murphy" by Nick and Charles Kenny; "I'm Calling You," by a group that called itself The Bridey Murphys; and "The Bridey Murphy Rock and Roll" ("Where are you Bridey Murphy?… Here I am… rockin' and rollin' with Kelly and Dolan and O'Callahan… Doin' the Bridey Murphy Rock and Roll").

Books on occultism, hypnosis, and reincarnation became mainstream hits—sales of one New Age publisher in Los Angeles reportedly multiplied by 25.

There was also at least one tragic episode. A 19-year-old Shawnee, Oklahoma newspaper carrier named Richard Swink shot himself dead after writing a note saying he was "curious about this Bridey Murphy story, so I am going to investigate the theory in person."

UNLIKE THE PUBLICITY-SHY Ginny Tighe, Morey reveled in the hoopla and celebrity notice. "Wherever we'd go, everybody wanted to meet the author of *Bridey Murphy*," according to Hazel, "and Morey ate up all that attention. We were invited out so much that it was hard to keep track of it all, and we had to turn down more invitations than we accepted."

The resulting social whirl introduced Morey and Hazel to luminaries of the literary and theater worlds. At one party, for example, Morey played one of the *Bridey* tapes for a group that included an orchestrator of the scores of numerous Broadway and Hollywood musicals. In the tape, Ginny sang a four-line tune as an example of a period Irish song, and the orchestrator wrote down a "score" for the tune that was actually used in the musical sequence of a movie a few months later.

In public, characteristically dressed in impeccable fashion (still the Sheik), Morey utilized his brilliance and charm to captivate gatherings with stories related to *Bridey* and to his broadening interests in the worlds of investments and parapsychology.

Endlessly, he sought out private audiences in which he could hold forth energetically and at length about the Bridey case. Most Friday nights, for example, he and Hazel attended meetings of an organization called the American Association for Research Enlightenment, after which he typically would invite as many as 30 of the attendees to their nearby apartment to hear his Bridey pitch.

Still, despite his thirst for acclaim—and despite his publisher's pleas and a growing tide of media requests—he absolutely refused to do live radio or television interviews, where control of the format and much of the subject matter would rest with others.

It was a significant foreboding of troubles to come. Amid the glamor and glitter, the traits that concerned the Lodge social worker would become increasingly manifest in the private life of what Morey's classmate would call a "control freak."

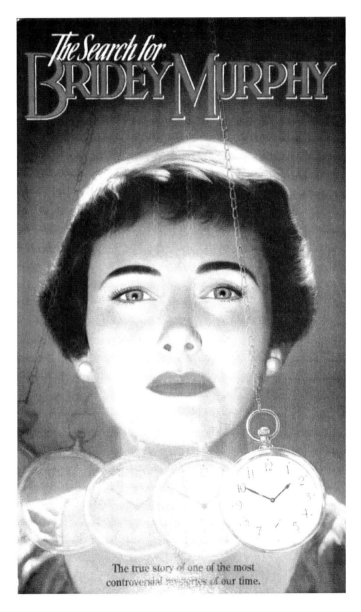

The movie, as it was later released on VHS

VII
"The 'F' Word... Things Like That"

FOR HAZEL, HER HUSBAND'S fame and success brought few advantages. Morey refused to move from their small one-bedroom apartment, where she sometimes felt like a visitor and even had trouble getting a good night's sleep. Many evenings, he would invite groups to the apartment to listen to him hold forth at length—but then he would go off to bed, and, as Hazel put it, "it would be up to me, alone, to take care of all those people."

Morey used the combination living room/dining room as his office, and often, when they had had no visitors, he would stay up much of the night—walking through the bedroom to the bathroom, turning lights off and on, and frequently coming to bed only to read. Hazel felt as though she needed to endlessly acclimate herself to what was rapidly becoming a bizarre lifestyle.

While avoiding any sort of gathering where he was not apt to be the center of attention, Morey took the allegiance of his friends—and his wife—for granted. He sometimes greeted visitors barefooted and in his undershorts. Unless they were there at his request to assist him in some way, he often ignored them, continuing whatever he was doing while leaving the social amenities to Hazel. When he did converse, his language was usually salted with obscenities and vulgarities, almost as though to cast a prosaic pallor over what the others might have to say.

The wife of a college friend of Morey's who lived nearby said she was often shocked when visiting Morey's apartment: "I wasn't used to hearing the cuss words he used. The 'F' word. 'Cunt.' Things like that. He gave me an education." She recalls him lying on the floor, ignoring his guests while restlessly clicking a TV remote, "just surfing the channels and cursing."

To an increasingly-frustrated Hazel, it was as though Morey's behavior was saying, "Look, here I am, I have all this money, I've written a bestseller, everyone wants me to be on their radio or TV program, I can run around in my dirty white undershorts in front of everyone and use all the filthy language I want, because everyone knows how intelligent I really am."

Further isolating Morey was his decision to stake his financial future on the investment techniques he was learning from his guru and colleague Benjamin Graham. Dollar-wise, it was a fruitful move. Over the next 40 years, his investment savvy would generate millions of dollars in profits. But it was a talent exercised almost entirely in private, analyzing corporate balance sheets and speaking on the telephone with corporate executives.

His fits of anger toward Hazel increased. He berated her, sometimes for hours, over matters as petty as complaints that she ran up the electric bill by failing to douse unneeded lights. Her personal journal indicates that his worst rages typically would begin with a tirade about my decision to leave the family business. As she recorded it, after a spell of denouncing me, he would he move on to excoriating her for a catalog of perceived faults.

By this time, of course, he had himself left the family business in Colorado. He was berating me for an act of supposed treason of which he too was guilty. And he continued to want me to join him in his *new* business.

Morey now considered himself the head of a one-man investment firm headquartered in New York, aided by his now-close relationship with Ben Graham. (He even enlisted Graham's help in finding financial backing for a parapsychological research project in which he was involved.)

At the Lodge, I heard none of Morey's criticism of me. What I did hear, via his telephone calls and visits during my early months at Chestnut Lodge, was increasing pressure for me to move to New York and join his investment activity there.

Meanwhile, Morey's "control freak" behavior was exacerbated by a public relations boomerang that soon branded him in the public mind as a dupe at best—and a charlatan at worst.

AMONG THOSE old enough to remember the *Bridey* craze, the reaction to its mention today is most likely to the effect of, "Oh, yeah. That was proved to be a hoax, or phony in some way, wasn't it?"

In fact, *Bridey* was smeared by an aggressive frenzy of facts-be-damned journalism.

Most of the early criticism of *Bridey* was, predictably, based on religious grounds. The notion of reincarnation was so obviously contrary to Catholic teachings, for example, that the Church did not even bother to place "Bridey" on its list of banned books. Explained a Catholic University of America theologian, Father Francis Connell of Chicago: "The general law of the Church forbids Catholics to read books that are opposed to the doctrines of the faith. This book would come under that general condemnation because it is opposed to the fundamental Christian doctrine according to which every individual has only one existence in this world, after which he will be rewarded or punished in accordance with the manner of life he has led." According to newspaper reports, Father Connell nevertheless discounted certain speculation within the Church that "the devil may have made use of the young woman's faculties while she was in a trance."

Most disconcerting among the early skeptics were various sensationalized "exposés" that blatantly pronounced the book and its author a "hoax"—on the basis, no less, of so-called "confessions" by Morey or Ginny. A Canadian magazine ran a large picture of Morey captioned, "Morey Bernstein hoaxed world with Search for Bridey Murphy." The accompanying text explained, "Only after he'd written a best-seller did Bernstein shamefacedly admit that *The Search for Bridey Murphy* belonged on the fiction, not the non-fiction, shelves." And a Chicago newspaper boldly claimed that an "exposed Bridey Murphy admitted her story was a hoax."

The explosive word "hoax," moreover, bannered in numerous headlines above stories that in fact made no such claim. A magazine of the era, *Top Secret*, ran a lengthy story, for example, sensationally captioned "Exposed: The Great Bridey Murphy Hoax." It contained a paragraph high in the text stating that Morey "has been called a fraud, a headline-seeking quack, a candidate for the padded cell… a sort of modern witch, who should be burned at the stake." But the story as a whole—to the rare reader who might read it all and could shake the effect of the headline's bias—eventually presented a balanced picture of the book and of Morey as patently sincere, though perhaps overly eager to accept "Bridey's" tale as literal gospel. (Which, indeed, is how I might best describe my own attitude toward my brother's book.)

Then, five months after the book's publication, a Hearst tabloid, the *Chicago American*, delivered the *coup de grâce*—a shaft from the quiver of yellow journalism that dimmed the book's status for decades. The *American's* claim—allegedly based on interviews with people who had known Ginny as a child—was that her statements under hypnosis were simply recollections of things she had seen and been told in the early years of her current lifetime. The theory was sufficiently reasonable on its face that even Morey was at first disinclined to dismiss it out of hand.

The debunking reports were widely reprinted. *Life* magazine, with its then-vast circulation, was among those that accepted the "findings" without question. Proclaimed *Life*, "Last week the search for Bridey Murphy was ended by a series of *Chicago American* articles."

In fact, the *American* series was without merit. One of its principal sources, for example, was a clergyman wrongly represented to have been the pastor of a church Ginny attended as a child. And the most important source was a childhood neighbor with whom Ginny had no recollection of any personal involvement—and who turned out to be the mother of the *American's* Sunday editor! However, the publicity generated by the articles, together with the numerous "hoax" reports, fatally condemned *Bridey* in much of the common view.

Ironically, the same *Life* magazine that had so cavalierly run the obituary of "the search" in 1956 would, however belatedly, resurrect it in 1988. Then, in a Time-Life Books publication, *Psychic Voyages*, Bridey Murphy was described as "the quintessential example of a previous life revealed by hypnotic regression" and cited respected scientists as saying Ginny's memories appeared to be "paranormal" and of "unexplained" origin.

One of those scientists was Dr. Ian Stevenson, Carlson Professor of Psychiatry at the University of Virginia. After resigning as chief of psychiatry at the university's medical school, Dr. Stevenson spent more than half a century investigating paranormal events that appear to suggest the existence of prior lives. As a general matter, he dismissed as unconvincing most accounts of past lives by hypnotic subjects, but his skepticism did not extend to the case of Bridey Murphy. He believed that some sort of paranormal influence was at work in the six Bridey sessions, citing various details provided by Ginny about early 19th-century Ireland that were later verified only by intensive research.

In Ginny's 1995 obituary, the *New York Times* stated: "The notion that the book was an out-and-out hoax never gained much credence for several reasons. Mr. Bernstein, for example, was a wealthy and highly-respected Pueblo businessman… His hypnosis sessions with Mrs. Morrow [Ginny's married name at death]…were conducted in front of respected witnesses who vouched for the apparent authenticity of Mrs. Morrow's regression. Also, Mrs. Morrow…seemed an entirely guileless subject. She insisted that her real name not be used in the book, which called her Ruth Simmons, and then shunned virtually every opportunity to cash in on the Bridey Murphy phenomenon."

Unfortunately, the resurrection of Bridey among careful investigators—unlike the "hoax" stories—was never widely publicized, and Morey would spend much of more than 30 years in foredoomed warfare against the debunkers.

His personal conviction of the validity of Bridey's reportage never faltered. In his personal vernacular, for example, people didn't "die." Rather, they had "gone to Brideyville."

VIII
The Road To Pinel

MY FIRST BREAKDOWN AND hospitalization had occurred in 1951, six years before my confinement at Pinel and Chestnut Lodge, triggered by my impending college graduation and the article of faith that I would join the family business. In retrospect, it's evident that my torment stemmed from my instinctive submission to Morey's need to be ever in total control of his personal world, and my conviction that I was hopelessly incapable of performing to his standards in the business world. I saw no way out of a hopeless dilemma, and the waves of thinly-dammed terror and anxiety overwhelmed me. Returning home from college for summer vacation, just one academic quarter shy of graduation, I lay in the back seat of my car, virtually paralyzed with panic and depression, while two friends did the driving.

Apparently forewarned by them that something was wrong, my parents were waiting in the living room, concern on their faces, when I arrived home and blurted out, "I'm crazy!"

Mother responded (in kind, as it were) by throwing herself on the floor and wailing shrilly as she rolled across the carpet, while Dad simply looked puzzled. A few days later, as Morey and Mother were discussing my condition with a Colorado Springs psychiatrist, I leapt from an anteroom window of the office onto a lawn three stories below. I blacked out, though surprisingly incurring nothing more physically serious than a slight ankle sprain, and woke up in Morey's car on my way to a local sanitarium.

The good news (besides the astonishingly-trivial injury) was that I was then somehow able to both convey my distaste for joining the business and elicit reluctant support from Morey and my father for what they privately considered my rank disloyalty. The bad news was that a few weeks in the sanitarium and a series of electric shock treatments failed to quell my depression for very long.

I managed nevertheless to return to Palo Alto to complete my final undergraduate term and begin therapy with a psychoanalyst, Dr. Don Jackson. As the end of term neared, still desperately anxious, I consulted a friendly professor about what I might do next. He suggested what should have been obvious—but which somehow had never occurred to me.

He pointed out that I had done well as a campus journalist—so why not apply with the local newspaper, the *Palo Alto Daily Times*? I did so, was hired, and after a few months became the paper's full-time political reporter. I worked there for the next five years, during which I also took graduate courses in Stanford's journalism department.

With the *Times*, in addition to politics, my beat covered Santa Clara County, including meetings of the Board of Supervisors and Planning Commission, the sheriff's department, and newsworthy courthouse trials.

During those years with the *Times*, I seemed to be making reasonable progress toward establishing independence from my brother and family. But inwardly, the anxieties rumbled on.

Expressions of approval from my editors and colleagues would only temporarily relieve either my conviction of ineptitude or the deeper sense of impending doom. At times, I even fantasized that Morey had worked out some arrangement with the publisher to hire me and keep me on. When the dean of the university's journalism school urged me to apply for a position with a big-city daily or national magazine, I froze in fear at the suggestion.

Finally, in what I would later see as simple retreat, I left the job and enrolled in a doctoral program in the university's English department. In effect, I yearned for the imagined peace and safety of the ivory tower.

BACK ON CAMPUS, two abortive love affairs helped dissolve my thin coating of composure and loosen the clouds of despair.

The first was a relationship of several months with Sally, a graduate journalism student with whom I came the closest I had ever known to genuine happiness. Our times together filled me with a curious, heretofore wholly-alien, sense of joy and lightness. But when she prepared to leave for a 10-day hometown vacation and questioned me closely about my plans for the future, I found myself unable to respond in anything but vague terms. When she returned, I discovered the full significance of her questioning and the heavy price of my hesitation: looking for commitment, she had succumbed to the pleadings of her undergraduate boyfriend—whom she had mentioned several times, to which I had paid little heed—and now wore his ring.

A few months later, on the rebound, I was involved with another young woman, Wendy, who dealt my ego a perhaps even more crushing blow. In the interest of openness, I told her about my bouts with depression—and she immediately broke off our relationship. Her father had similar difficulties, she said, and she was unwilling to risk the kind of agony that it had meant for her mother.

Wendy and I had been seeing each other several times a week, but now she refused to even take my telephone calls. To me, the rebuff felt like far more than mere rejection: it rekindled my deepest and darkest fears, confirming my secret belief that I was ultimately doomed by my craziness to permanent abandonment and isolation. I sank into a state of wretched desperation and anguished withdrawal.

I had only recently enrolled in the doctoral program, and as yet knew few people there. Facing a lengthy Christmas vacation with no plans and few meaningful relationships, the anguish mounted. I had no appetite for food. I couldn't sleep. I couldn't concentrate sufficiently to read a book or follow a television program. Though unbearably lonely, I panicked at the thought of the most trivial social interaction.

I had spent six years attempting to carve out a measure of autonomy, to shed my pervasive sense of helplessness and find a life beyond the shadow of a dynamic and charismatic brother. Now, tellingly, it was to him that I turned for rescue.

IX
...And On To The Lodge

IN DESPERATION, AND TO the dismay of Dr. Jackson, I telephoned Morey. The next evening, he and his wife Hazel flew in from New York where they were then living. The following morning in Dr. Jackson's Palo Alto office, the four of us discussed my plight.

Despite my lifelong qualms about becoming a mental patient (symbolized by a dreaded childhood image of the Colorado State Hospital), my admission to Pinel was actually of my own doing. As we talked in Dr. Jackson's office, I said that I longed for some quiet neutral ground where I could make a fresh start, and I asked Dr. Jackson if he knew of any hospital that might provide that for me.

He suggested Chestnut Lodge, where he had done a residency—and for me, the name alone conjured visions (ironically, as it turned out) of a restful woodland retreat, sparking a flash of hope. But upon telephoning there, Dr. Jackson was told that the Lodge had no vacant beds. The next best, he said, was a place in Seattle called Pinel—so he called there and arranged for my admission. He described Pinel as a small, elite hospital founded by doctors trained at the famed Menninger Clinic and situated on the semi-rural, pine-studded northeast edge of Seattle.

Morey, Hazel, and I flew there that evening—arriving in Seattle at midnight, and checking into a 12th-floor room at the Olympic Hotel. Morey, obviously concerned, worriedly referred to the outcome of my breakdown six-and-a-half years before. Now I stood at the hotel room window and thought there could be no question that twelve stories to pavement—unlike that earlier three-story leap to grass—would do the job. I stifled the image. But my panic grew.

Hazel's diary for the next day contains the notation: "Went to Pinel about two. Bob immediately taken to room. We couldn't go… Pinel seems all right, but who knows. As Bob got out of cab when we arrived, he said, 'Hazel, please don't give up on me.'…It is terribly hard for him. Poor tormented soul."

I arrived at Pinel intensely anxious and depressed but still (however shakily) in some degree of self-control. But within days, not to put too fine a point on it, I had become an unmanageable fruitcake.

A PINEL AIDE escorted me not to my room, as Hazel thought, but to a ward lounge—where I sat, alone, for what seemed an eternity, panic turning to pulse-pounding terror. I saw other patients walking about, talking and laughing, but no one spoke to me. Finally, the aide returned and showed me to a bed in a dormitory-like arrangement. Another aide brought food on a tray, but I couldn't eat. Nor, all that night, could I sleep. The next morning, a doctor who said his name was Iverson asked if I had had any thoughts about suicide. I admitted that I had, and within hours I was transferred to the closed ward and placed on suicide precautions.

After spending years struggling to gain a sense of independence from Morey, only to turn to him at a time of high crisis, my ambivalence now took yet another perverse turn: I told Dr. Iverson I didn't want to see Morey. So Iverson asked him to leave Seattle immediately. (I would learn some years later that Iverson did so willingly and perhaps even eagerly. He and his superior had immediately suspected something amiss between Morey and me. As one of them expressed it to a colleague, his first intuitive impression was "of something being really involved and sick" in the relationship.)

On the locked ward, the suicide precautions were basically synonymous with solitary confinement. My small bedroom and a tiny ward lounge became my entire world. My eyeglasses were taken away whenever a nurse, aide, or doctor was not at my immediate side. Meals came on trays brought to the room. My foggy vision cast an eerie, unreal aura about my little cell. By the second afternoon, the tension unbearable, I found myself uncontrollably banging my head against the headboard of my bed crying, "No, no, no" and "Please, please, please." (Please what? Please help me? Please relieve the tension? Please get me out of here? I don't know.) Aides removed the bed for the night, leaving me with only the mattress on the floor.

The constant fuss about my glasses and the long hours of vision-shrouded inactivity and isolation took a heavy toll. At first, I didn't understand why everyone was so concerned about my eyeglasses. When I finally did get the message—that they could be used as a weapon—my "reasoning" took a darkly paranoid turn. I decided the staff were trying to tell me I was beyond hope, in effect that I was better off dead, and were suggesting one means of accomplishing it.

The following days were a blur of bizarre behavior on my part: attempting to "drown" myself in a few inches of water draining from a bathtub, with an aide just a few feet away… trying to "strangle" myself by stuffing the corner of a pillow in my mouth… poking a spoon or a cigarette at my eye (but somehow always missing)… spending more and more time in restraints, lying on my bed with my arms strapped down (but still managing to inflict light cuts to my right wrist by rubbing it against the bedside)… putting the lit end of a cigarette in my mouth after picking at a meal brought by an aide… being forced like an invalid to use a bedpan in my room (forbidden by formal order from using the communal bathroom)… becoming temporarily even-more confused as a result of three electric shock treatments.

Finally, I decided to become genuinely serious about ending my life: no more theatrics until circumstances allowed me to do it successfully. I set about to convince the staff that, beyond hope or not, I no longer wanted to hurt myself. It worked. After a few days, I was given permission to wear my glasses in the lounge unaccompanied.

ON THE MORNING of December 23, 1957, I slipped from the lounge into my bedroom, broke a lens, and cut my wrists with one of the shards of glass. With my strength and consciousness ebbing, I also managed three clumsy swipes at my neck. (As a reporter, some months before, I had covered the trial of a man who killed his wife and then sliced his own wrists and neck. Copycat?) The ward's chief nurse found me a few minutes later and administered first aid while others called for an ambulance. According to the nurse who drew the bedside duty in the general hospital where I was taken for transfusion and surgery, my first words to him on waking (of which I have no memory) were hardly those of gratitude: "Why did you save me, you son of a bitch?"

Back at Pinel, it was clear that my violence had panicked the staff. For 26 days, not a single aide or nurse was willing to tend to me out of shackles, other than to allow me to take meals from a tray, to occasionally smoke a cigarette, and to relieve myself in a bedpan.

What a Pinel doctor understated in a formal progress note as an "undercurrent of distrust" mandated my departure from Pinel. The moment a bed became available at the Lodge, Pinel arranged for my transfer.

And so I landed at Chestnut Lodge and got my introduction to the Dantean Third Floor. As I saw it at that point, I had traded solitary confinement for a veritable snake pit—a horror-movie model of a madhouse.

DAWN OF MY FIRST DAY at the Lodge brought a change of shift and a new Special who introduced himself as Ernest. As he helped me bathe and dress (a process complicated by the wrist dressings and unwieldy casts), I learned, among other things, that he was Jamaican, and working there part-time while studying for a Master's degree at a nearby Seventh Day Adventist college. (But

I apparently missed a lot, too. In a subsequent nursing station conference, Ernest would report about me, "He's not always aware when you say something to him.")

In the hallway, the usual commotion prevailed. At Pinel, where I had been kept in restraints most of the time, I had hardly even been aware of other patients—with one ghastly exception: when I lay shackled to my bed forced to listen for extended periods of time to the piercing screams of a woman across the hall, who seemed to be in the throes of some excruciating torture. I never encountered her in person, but I would later learn that she succeeded in strangling herself to death some days later.

Henry stood in a corner, his arms raised, turning slowly, endlessly, round and round, to his left; I wondered how he could keep from at least periodically resting his arms. The morning greeting of the "Mafia Man" consisted of another stream of incomprehensible invective. The pudgy man, no longer complaining of his bowels—perhaps he'd visited the bathroom?—now paced back and forth along one side of the hallway, repeatedly muttering something that sounded like, "Bah, fongu." Glancing in a bedroom door, I saw a young man standing just inside, his pants open, masturbating. Ernest spied him and said sharply, "Stop that, Albert, or get inside your room!" (I would learn that Albert's father was one of the world's most famous statesmen.) A large man I hadn't noticed before was seated in a chair holding a plastic glass: repetitively, he emptied his false teeth into the glass, replaced them in his mouth, spit them back into the glass—and so on and on. Two other men (I thought of them as the pacers) seemed in perpetual motion, walking back and forth, back and forth, 12 or 15 steps at a time.

Another patient I noticed for the first time seemed out of place in the bizarre surroundings. About 40 years old, of medium height and build, with cropped mustache and neatly-tended brown hair, he wore a fresh white dress shirt and pressed woolen slacks, and wholly lacked the generally-disheveled look of the others. To my surprise he approached smiling, offered a handshake, and told me his name was Jeffrey. He spoke in a confident tone.

"You must be the new patient," he said. "It's good to see you. We don't get many here who can carry on a conversation."

I mumbled something about not being all that confident of my own capacity in that regard. But I found his presence momentarily reassuring. Raving lunacy, however ubiquitous, apparently was not a hard and fast requirement for admission to the Third Floor. (Binge violence, it seemed, would suffice: I would learn that in the real world, Jeffrey had been a psychiatrist in a Western state, committed here after a diagnosis of psychosis freed him of criminal charges arising from the beating of a girlfriend.)

Before we could speak further, one of the pacers stopped before me, thrust out his chin, and said, "Are you crazy? If you're not, they'll make you that way here pretty quick."

I froze at his words. It was as though he was reading my thoughts. How could anyone stay sane, much less become sane, in this atmosphere?

I watched Henry twirl, Albert masturbate, the Mafia Man rant, and the pacers pace. And I wondered in desperation: Why should one hospital succeed where another had failed?

X

Bourbon, Haircut, And A Shrinking Shrink

As my memories of Pinel deepened the desperation engendered by the bed-lam around me, I retreated to my bedroom, tailed by Ernest, my shadow of the moment. Shortly, a young doctor of about my age came to the door, introduced himself as Dr. Gibson, and greeted me with an engaging smile and easy manner. Emboldened by his relaxed ways, I told him of Henry's attempt to relieve himself on my head and asked if I could room with Jeffrey instead. To my surprise, he immediately agreed, though he said the arrange-ments would involve some other switches and might take a few days. I also complained about water leaking from the ceiling in one corner of the room. He said it probably was from a plumbing problem on the Fourth Floor ward and should be fixed by the end of the day.

He asked how I had slept and I told him, truthfully, not at all. I added that before my breakdown, as a matter of routine, I had drunk a small amount of bourbon each night at bedtime to help get me to sleep, and that I really did miss that.

"Have you ever had a drinking problem?" he asked. "No," I said. He paused a moment, and then stunned me once more: "We'll see about getting a bottle for you. We can keep it in the nursing station, and I'll write up an order for you to be given a shot of bourbon at night."

What a nutty nuthouse, I thought. The inmates might not be running the asylum, but they did seem to have a vote. Even more startling, after my experiences of the past weeks, the doctor had actually taken me at my word and accepted my denial of alcoholism.

Well, why not go for broke. So I raised the matter of a haircut, which at Pinel had become a major, ongoing, festering source of irritation. The period featured neatly cropped men's hairstyles, and I had entered Pinel nearly seven weeks earlier even then in need of a trim. By late December my hair was long and unruly, sharpening my already repellent self-image. I had pleaded with the Pinel personnel to be escorted to a barber shop or, alternatively, to pay for a barber to come to the locked ward. They would have none of it. Daunted by my earlier violence, they refused to allow me beyond the heavy doors of their locked ward and were indifferent to assurances that I would behave. And hospital procedures simply contained no provision for importing barbers. My anger at their refusal, they implied, was just another symptom of my derangement.

But when I told Dr. Gibson I wanted a haircut, he just nodded. "Sure," he said. "Earl can go with you to a barber shop in Rockville. It's less than a mile away. How about this afternoon?"

That was it. A simple matter handled in a simple way. Maybe there were advantages to being in a *real* loony bin. People here acted as though they'd seen it all. My own craziness seemed of no great moment.

"The county liquor store is near the barber shop," Dr. Gibson added. "Maybe you can pick up a fifth of bourbon while you're there."

I remembered my nervousness the night before at Normandie Farm, and hoped I could organize myself to deal with "normal" people on the outside.

WHEN DR. GIBSON LEFT, Ernest escorted me down three flights of stairs for breakfast in a large, noisy yellow-lighted basement room that functioned as a cafeteria. The food line included both men and women of all ages, some staring fixedly, others prancing and gabbling, many being helped by aides with their food. At one table, two women screamed at each other. At others, people chattered, whether in conversation or competing monologues I couldn't tell.

We set our trays at a table with two of the men I had noticed the evening before on the Third Floor. One, a tall, powerful-looking man, leapt from a chair, cried "Ernest," and wrapped my companion in a vigorous embrace that seemed like something between affectionate hug and personal attack. Apparently neither surprised nor ruffled, Ernest simply said, "Good morning, Glen," and we sat down.

I nodded to both strangers and introduced myself. Glen responded with a sort of haughty sniff, reached into a shirt pocket, extracted a card, and handed it to me. Its engraved letters read, "Glen Staple, Concert Pianist and Horse Trainer." I nodded as though impressed, uncertain what to say.

"Are you a friend or an enemy?" he asked.

"Well, uh—a friend."

"I think you're a homosexual pervert. You're angry with me, crazy, out of control. I can't trust you."

Ernest spared me. "Take it easy, Glen," he said. "Enjoy your breakfast, and we'll talk about it later."

Our other tablemate was a slender scholarly-looking man with a bemused, enigmatic half-smile who didn't respond when I told him my name. Ernest said this was Max, but my "Hi, Max" again drew no response. I gave up and focused edgily on my plate of scrambled eggs and toast.

As we were leaving, I noticed Jeffrey eating and talking at a table with two attractive young women. The younger one, in particular, caught my attention: she was pert, shapely, and dark-haired, perhaps in her early twenties.

On the way up the stairs, I asked Ernest about the women. He said the younger one was Laura, and the other Bonnie. They were patients on the Second Floor, a semi-open women's ward, as distinguished from the Fourth Floor, a locked equivalent of my own men's ward. Both women, he said, had serious addiction problems.

In my resolve to divert myself from my seething anxieties, I asked if there were any games available. Ernest found a jigsaw puzzle and we sat at a small table in the hallway outside my room. We hadn't been working at it long when Dr. Gibson came to our table with a woman he introduced as Dr. Sokoloff, my therapist-to-be. It was time for our first session.

Dr. Sokoloff and I went into my room and sat on two wooden chairs in one corner. I asked her for a match (Third Floor patients weren't allowed to carry them), which she gave me, and I lit both our cigarettes. She put the matches between us where I could reach them when needed, and I silently thanked her for the gesture. She was of medium height, slender build, dark brown mid-length hair, brown eyes, delicate features, and a tentative, almost shy manner. It was difficult to tell which of us was the more nervous one. Was she frightened, I wondered, because of my record of violence? Our mutual uneasiness grew when patients fighting outside the door distracted us on two occasions.

She told me she'd be seeing me for 40 minutes four times a week, but that today she'd stay a little longer to give us a chance to get to know each other.

"I don't know where to start," I told her. "I suppose you already know a lot about me."

"Not very much. I prefer hearing it from you."

And so, I talked (or perhaps more accurately, rambled) about various aspects of my past: my earlier suicide attempt, my treatment with Don Jackson, my work with the Palo Alto newspaper, my frustrations with my doctoral program. Cautiously, I edged into the events of the past few months:

my inability to work or even read, my escalating fears of being alone, my decision to call Morey, the horrific events at Pinel.

She asked my reaction to being at the Lodge, and I told her some of my thoughts about Dr. Jackson—that he must have recommended the Lodge because he figured I was really sick, like the loonies all around me. I said they made me feel creepy and frightened, especially the Mafia Man and Glen Staples, who had seemed ready to attack me as some sort of imagined "homosexual pervert." I gave her a laundry list of what I saw as some of the Lodge's more objectionable qualities.

I guessed the doctor to be a few years older than my age of 31. I was both drawn to and given pause by her demure, low-key manner. As she left, I wondered: Was this restrained, soft-spoken woman (sort of a shrinking shrink, I thought) up to the task of helping lift me out of a pathologic quagmire? Was she frightened by me?

On this muted, questioning note, began one of the most important and rewarding (if sometimes stormy) emotional relationships of my life.

AT THE APPOINTED TIME, Earl showed up to spell Ernest, and we set off on a trip that netted me a haircut and a fifth of bourbon, plus a round-trip stroll along the postcard-classic village street known as West Montgomery Avenue that I had glimpsed from the cab the day before. Earl, as I observed then, was neither the most garrulous nor most handsome of men. But he was plainly far from the sadist that he had first seemed. In fact, I would soon learn that among staff and patients alike, he was perhaps the most respected and well-liked of the sixty-plus Lodge aides.

As we walked he seldom spoke, but managed to impart a bit of Rockville history. He mentioned, for example, that both the author Scott Fitzgerald and his wife Zelda were buried in Rockville Cemetery. When we reached Washington Street, downtown Rockville's three-block main thoroughfare and the site of its sole barber shop, Earl pointed out the old courthouse with its statue of a Confederate soldier. During the Civil War, he said, Rockville had actually harbored both Union and Confederate sympathizers, and the courthouse was used at different times by both sides as a temporary hospital for the wounded.

In the shop, the barber greeted Earl by name—which I took as a clear sign that the barber would know I was a Lodge patient. A *crazy*. But his manner was matter-of-fact, and as he clipped away he commented on the clear, brisk weather. I mumbled some self-conscious replies and felt relief when he was finished.

Earl walked me a few doors down the street to the liquor store. I paid for a bottle of Early Times and was struck once again by the seeming incongruity—my personal, prescribed flagon of booze to stow in the asylum.

Back on the Third Floor, the ward now had a different feel—not quite so scary. The haircut, so long withheld, was welcome. Amid the pacing and groaning and screaming in the ward, I could picture what lay just outside: a pleasant, sleepy, proud little edge-of-the-Old-South town. And I knew I could go there again, perhaps, as I had that day, just for the asking.

Two student nurses were on duty, and one of them was the brown-haired, brown-eyed young woman with the electrifying smile from the afternoon before. She approached me timidly and spoke in a soft, rich drawl.

"Nurse George asked me to change the dressing on your wrists."

I held out each of my arms in turn and she unwrapped the ace bandages from the half casts, tended to the wrists, and strapped the casts back in place. Watching her pleasant features as she worked, I became unaware for a moment of my haunting anxieties. When she was finished, I asked her about herself. As it turned out, her name, Pat Brown, matched her eyes and hair. In her engaging accent, she told me she was from Charlotte, North Carolina, and in training there at Presbyterian Hospital.

Nervously, as if it were an invitation to the junior prom, I asked if she could play a game of cards or chess with me.

"I'm sorry, Miss George has other things for me to do." She smiled wistfully and managed to inject a note of regret into her delightful inflections.

IN ADDITION TO the outside stairway accessible only through the bolted iron door at the end of the hall, a second, interior flight of stairs provided direct passage among the three ward floors. The stairwell was encased, however, and generally barred on each floor by locked wooden doors. Now I would discover that the doors between the Second and Third Floors were opened during evening hours—creating, some years ahead of its time, a sort of part-time coed dormitory.

Shortly after returning from dinner in the cafeteria, I was sitting in the lounge with my latest Special, who told me his name was Jiggs. To my surprise, Laura and Bonnie, the lively young patients who had drawn my attention in the cafeteria, came rushing in, followed by a slower-paced Jeffrey.

"We want to meet the new patient," Bonnie said. "Jeffrey says you have some of your marbles."

Bonnie and I discovered that we were in a sense neighbors: her home was in Atherton, California, an elite residential enclave near Palo Alto, where I had been living and working in recent years. Laura, so garrulous in the cafeteria, now seemed somewhat shy, but I did learn that she had lived for some time with her parents in Paris.

As Laura and Jeffrey walked hand-in-hand to a corner sofa and huddled in seemingly-intimate conversation, Bonnie challenged me to a game of Scrabble. Her play was spirited and competitive, providing some of the distraction I craved (though I found it difficult to avoid glancing at Laura, snuggling and laughing with Jeffrey nearby).

The Lodge, while no rose garden, was no padded cell either. Being crazy, it seemed, wasn't necessarily the end of the world.

But crazy I was, and with the credentials to prove it. Forty years later, I recovered from Lodge files a copy of the "State of Maryland…Commitment

Certificate." The heart of the document was a bald statement signed by a Dr. George Sharpe, a general practitioner I remembered examining me a few days after my arrival: "I do hereby certify…and do believe that the said Robert Allen Bernstein is insane."

XI

Behind The Scenes: "A World-Class Complainer"

AFTER DR. GIBSON'S FIRST meeting with me, he commented in a tape-recorded staff meeting that I seemed at times on the verge of tears, "as though looking around, he felt he must have reached the end of the road." The admitting physician noted in his report that "Bob certainly shows evidence of severe depression." But despite my apparent sadness, Dr. Gibson further reported that he detected no overt hint of suicidal behavior and that he found me quite coherent.

The night shift nursing report recorded Henry's show of inhospitality, and noted that Dr. Gibson had already decided to move me to another room. But Henry's behavior was just one of a long string of noted grievances that I voiced to aides and to Dr. Gibson: among other things, the noise, draftiness, uncomfortable mattress, water leaking through the ceiling, and my need for a haircut.

Dr. Gibson decided that while my therapist would investigate what lay behind the grumpiness, for now, well... maybe a bedtime shot of liquor would help. And the haircut request provided an opportunity for what he called "lengthening the leash." Dr. Gibson was confident that Earl was capable of handling any problems that might possibly develop.

Dr. Gibson paid little heed to the fact that Pinel had classified me as schizophrenic. Today, with a broad panoply of available drugs, careful diagnosis can be important. In the nearly-drugless 1950s, however, the label had little if any influence on the approach to treatment. Moreover, since the Lodge was then known as a hospital of last resort, referring hospitals almost always labeled patients being transferred there as schizophrenic. Schizophrenia was then viewed as essentially hopeless—and hence, as Dr. Gibson put it, such a label "served as adequate explanation for the patients' failure to improve at their own institutions."

Nevertheless, he now found me—as would Dr. Sokoloff a few hours later—to be "something of a world-class complainer."

STILL, DR. GIBSON had to admit to himself that at least one of my complaints—about the leakage—had merit.

"Oh, oh!" he thought. "Mitzi's at it again."

Mitzi was a patient on the women's locked ward on the Fourth Floor. She had been at the Lodge for 10 years following lengthy hospitalizations elsewhere. She was educated in Europe and spoke several languages fluently. (One Lodge therapist complained that in the midst of a therapy session she sometimes burst into a stream of French, which he didn't understand.) Though seemingly only mildly psychotic, and capable of considerable charm and wit, she was now confined to the Fourth Floor because she was also capable of angry, sometimes assaultive, outbursts.

In those outbursts, she regularly plugged up the Lodge drainage system by flushing underwear down the Fourth Floor toilet. Employees who worked on the Fourth Floor knew they would occasionally need to rush into the communal bathroom with a coat hanger to pull a bra or pair of panties out of one of the toilets—but sometimes they arrived too late to prevent some flooding.

Occasionally, the Mitzi-induced plumbing problems extended beyond the Lodge. In one instance, when a major portion of the entire town's sewage system had been shut down, a frustrated sanitation worker had marched into the office of a red-faced Lodge administrator, gingerly holding up the source of the stoppage—an outsized brassiere. Another time, midway through dinner at Normandie Farm, no less, with aide Jiggs Kovin and another patient, Mitzi excused herself to visit the women's room: when she returned, Jiggs could see her once-firmly encased bosom now bouncing freely inside her blouse. He quickly called for the check—and was embarrassed (though not surprised) to see a cascade of water flow from under the women's room door, into the elegantly carpeted foyer through which they exited.

Some years later, after Dr. Gibson became head of Sheppard Pratt Institute in Baltimore, Mitzi transferred to that hospital—where she no longer exhibited the need to dispose of her underwear in such fashion. As Dr. Gibson would write the then-head of Chestnut Lodge, "We don't know whether we have better therapy, or better plumbing."

FOR SOME YEARS, Mitzi's therapist at the Lodge had been Frieda Fromm-Reichmann. Though less well-known to the general public than her ex-husband, psychiatrist and best-selling author Erich Fromm, Dr. Fromm-Reichmann brought the Lodge considerable professional stature as a graduate of the Berlin Institute, the former director of a Heidelberg psychiatric hospital, and a student of Sigmund Freud himself.

In the 1960s, Fromm-Reichmann would be immortalized in print and film as the kindly, masterful "Dr. Fried" in *I Never Promised You a Rose Garden*, a classic fictionalized account of a young woman's actual treatment and recovery at the Lodge. (As I write, the frame structure known as Frieda's Cottage, where Dr. Fromm-Reichman lived and saw patients, is the sole remaining Lodge building, and the National Park Service has expressed interest in nominating the Cottage as a National Historic Landmark.)

Frieda Fromm-Reichmann

Fromm-Reichmann felt that if she could establish any sort of relationship, on whatever possible basis, good could come. If this meant walking, stooped-over, in an attempt to communicate with a young woman wrapped in a rug rolling down a hospital corridor—or, as in *I Never Promised You A Rose Garden*, role-playing in patient Deborah's imaginary land of "Yr" and its cast of jealous and demanding gods—well, so be it.

Fromm-Reichmann always saw Mitzi in Mitzi's room, and because Mitzi always sat on the floor, Fromm-Reichmann would join her there during their sessions. But one day Mitzi suggested that "it would really be much more proper" for the doctor to sit in a chair. Pleased that Mitzi seemed to be conveying a feeling of respect, the doctor moved into a nearby bowl-shaped plastic chair. To the sound of a muted squish and some immediate personal discomfort, she quickly realized that Mitzi's expressed concern for protocol had been a sly gambit. Mitzi had prepared for the doctor's daily visit by urinating in the chair.

IN KEEPING WITH Dr. Fromm-Reichmann's personalized theory of treatment, Lodge doctors usually dressed casually, avoiding the suits and ties more typical of the breed. Visitors might have had some difficulty distinguishing between staff and some of the better-groomed patients. This was brought home to one new psychiatrist when he was looking for a rental apartment where his family could live while they looked for a house. Told that the head social worker kept a file of available short-term rentals, he knocked on her door and stated his request. She looked at him somewhat skeptically and replied, "It isn't usual, you know, for someone to start out as an outpatient."

That doctor had no difficulty adapting to the Lodge's ways. Before long, he might take a patient for a ride on the Potomac River in his amphibious vehicle, or to his home for dinner. At one such dinner, a patient named Fred put out his cigarette in a serving bowl of vegetables. The doctor told Fred that was something he shouldn't do again—whereupon the doctor's 10-year-old son corrected his father: "Dad, he's a guest. We don't tell guests what to do."

My scholarly-looking, mute breakfast mate Max was indeed a scholar, reputed to be one of the world's five most-gifted mathematicians. Although I never heard him speak, it was clear that on some esoteric plane, his brain continued to function at a high level.

As a professor of mathematics at Stanford, Max Shiffman's work had been crucial to the development of the airfoil design that first made supersonic flight possible. As I would later learn, three major corporations were funding his stay at the Lodge as a hopeful investment in his scientific genius.

Frieda's Cottage in 2018, at the Chestnut Lodge Park

At one point, a Defense Department scientist came to Dr. Gibson seeking help from Max with a weaponry problem. Their own mathematicians, he said, had been unable to sufficiently reduce the number of variables in a key equation to render it digestible by the era's cumbersome early-stage computers. Gibson authorized the visit but warned the scientist that no one had been able to hold an intelligible conversation with Max in months. Undaunted, the scientist proceeded into Max's room and stayed an hour or so, writing formulas on a portable blackboard. Afterward, he reported that while Max hadn't said anything, he did seem to pay attention and looked as though he might have understood.

The same scientist returned six weeks later. Max's psychotic state had continued and no one on the ward had seen him reading or writing. But when the visitor came out of Max's room, he was ecstatic—clutching a blackboard with some fresh equations chalked by Max.

"He's done it!" the man exclaimed. "He's reduced the variables to a workable number!"

Another time, his emotional state somewhat improved, Max gave Dr. Gibson a one-page "letter" he wanted to send to a prestigious think-tank publication. To Dr. Gibson, the page seemed little more than a collection of mathematical symbols. Perhaps it's just gibberish, he thought, and this could be embarrassing. So he sent it, but with what he hoped was a discreet cover letter explaining Max's current straits. He received a prompt reply from the editor declaring his delight and his intention to publish Max's letter in the next issue. Max, it seemed, had solved another classic problem that had been puzzling mathematicians for decades.

Max's uncanny retention of his mathematical ability while schizophrenic is something of a historical oddity, according to a 1998 biography of Nobel Prize winner John Nash. Nash himself was institutionalized in 1959, nine years after formulating the theorem that belatedly won him a Nobel Prize in 1994. His biographer, Sylvia Nasar, makes the point in *A Beautiful Mind* that outstanding mathematicians often have difficulty communicating with others and that schizophrenic episodes are not uncommon among their lot. But she cites Max as one of only two (Nash being the other) who have ever recovered their mathematics ability after a schizophrenic breakdown.

CLEARLY, IT WAS FITTING that Max should be formally committed as "insane." But why was I also? Dr. Gibson would explain to me how my commitment came about.

Under Maryland law, a voluntary patient could submit a request for discharge within three days, and if the hospital felt the patient might be a danger to himself or others, its only remedy would be to file a court suit to intervene. Hence, to avoid that messy and expensive complication, the Lodge under such circumstances would have the patient legally committed, which required filing the official state certification with its boilerplate language declaring the patient to be "insane." So the word that so offended me came from state law, not from Lodge staff.

But why, I wondered, had my certification been signed by a general practitioner rather than a psychiatrist? Dr. Gibson explained:

"By experience, we had learned that many judges were distrustful of psychiatrists—their view apparently being, 'Sure, *they* think *everybody* is crazy.' So we found it more prudent to use family physicians, even though by definition they were less familiar with the ailments they were certifying to."

XII

"Because You're Not All There"

FOR THE FIRST WEEK or so on the Third Floor, I pretty much heeded the advice of the peerless pitcher and phrasemaker Satchel Paige: "Don't look back. Something may be gaining on you." Despite largely-sleepless nights, my cumbersome arm casts, and what I feared was the hopelessness of my plight, I compulsively sought out distracting activities.

So it was, ironically, that the best thing I had going for me was my grim Pinel prognosis. The principal purpose of 24/7 specialing was of course to protect me from self-inflicted harm—but it also provided constant companionship and a significant degree of freedom. I could keep on the move, explore the 20-acre Lodge campus and the town of Rockville, shoot baskets with my guard of the moment in the Main Building's yard, or occupy my mind with card and board games. One aide, Dan, was a chess buff who taught me a game ideally-suited for someone seeking mental distraction.

I learned that the patient population was about 110, housed mostly in the Main Building, and at a rather-attractive two-story plantation-style residence known as Hilltop: an "open" unit where the patients had freedom to come and go. Along the winding road leading from Main to Hilltop, were a smaller "open" patient residence known as Little Lodge; an old barn reconstructed into staff offices and open areas for various activities; a modern brick building housing a student nurses' dormitory; a rambler-style, glassed-in structure known as The Center; and the modest white frame residence known as Frieda's Cottage—the residence of Dr. Fromm-Reichmann, where she had died some months before my arrival.

The Center, I was told, was the site of various recreation facilities, arts and crafts, social events, and group meetings. There, I met two attractive young recreational therapists, Judy Richardson and June Mazer. With their encouragement I briefly tried my hand at sketching and pottery-making—ill-fated efforts that merely reminded me of my lifelong ineptness at manual arts of any sort, and reinforced my embedded sense of helplessness.

Another tiny frame building, little more than a shed, was known as the Kiosk: a soda-and-sundries shop staffed by patients who could there earn the current minimum wage. My Special of the moment, the young man named Jiggs, told me that the Kiosk was only a few months old—built by the joint labor of patients and staff, including several of the doctors who turned out on weekends to work beside the patients: shoveling stone for the slab foundation, pounding nails, etc.

Within a few days, Dr. Gibson shifted the room assignments and moved me in with Jeffrey. Now I could actually talk with my roommate and expect a coherent reply. Jeffrey became a source of information about the histories and predilections of other patients and staff, which speeded my settling-in process.

In retrospect, it seems quite appropriate that on several occasions in those early days, a staffer or patient—introduced to me by my Special of the moment—would respond, "Oh, you're the brother of Morey Bernstein." Even in the nuthouse, it seemed, my identity was simply a reflection of my brother.

WHILE I PERSONALLY felt nothing but anger and fear toward my first roommate, I soon learned that some members of the staff felt quite differently about Henry. The aide Jiggs was one of them. When he was first hired and taken around to meet all the patients, Jiggs told me, Henry was lying stiff on his back, eyes staring fixedly off to the left, tongue hanging from the corner of his mouth. An aide introduced Jiggs: "Henry, this is Jiggs. He's new here, and you'll be seeing him from time to time." Henry remained absolutely motionless—not a flicker evident in his rigid body, his dangling tongue, or the glassy eyes seemingly focused on some imaginary point off to the side.

Jiggs was initially assigned to the Fourth Floor women's ward and didn't see Henry again for about three months, until one day the emergency bell summoned all Main Building aides to the Third Floor. There he found Henry thrashing wildly on the floor, with four or five aides frantically working to pin his arms and legs. As Jiggs grabbed one of his arms, Henry's head rolled toward Jiggs, he looked at the aide, and he plaintively uttered four of the few words he was ever heard to speak at the Lodge: "Don't hurt me, Jiggs." Jiggs was flabbergasted, awed that Henry knew his name, and from that moment felt a rather deep affection for the catatonic patient. Even when Henry acted his craziest, Jiggs said, "I get a feeling of friendliness."

Moreover, according to Jiggs, several of the aides shared his feelings of warmth for Henry: an ex-World War II paratrooper who, despite his cadaverous appearance, remained quite powerful. Jiggs told me, for example, that once—upon arrival with a vanload of patients and aides at a vacation house rented by the Lodge at Chesapeake Bay—Henry jumped from the car, raced down a wooden pier, shed his clothes as he ran, and leapt into the Bay. Desperate aides dived in after him, but were quickly outdistanced by Henry's powerful crawl stroke. To their relief, he eventually turned around, swam back to the pier, climbed out, dressed, and, without a word, relapsed into his catatonic ways.

Warm feelings toward their charges were actually quite common among the aides. Earl, for example—whose somber mien had frightened me when he escorted me to the Third Floor upon my arrival—turned out in fact to be innately gentle and understanding, and a comforting presence to patients. Earl didn't coddle patients, though: I once saw him kick a patient gently in the rump with the admonition, "Mr. Miller, you're supposed to stay in your room." And when one patient asked, "Why am I here?", Earl responded quite directly, "Because you're not all there."

Just like the rest of us, I thought.

IMPROBABLY, EARL SEEMED to have a special rapport with his direct boss, Chief Aide Bill Thomas, who by temperament, education, and background could not differ more sharply from Earl. Bill, I learned, had been a child actor—and as a young man, had worked off-Broadway with such then-unknowns as Marlon Brando and Kirk Douglas, before his own stage career was cut short by a brief psychotic episode that landed him in a ward at the Bellevue Mental Hospital. And while his experience there led him down a very different career path, theatricality clearly remained integral to his professional and personal style. He was friendly, open, and witty, and delighted in a sometimes outrageous (and often ribald) directness of manner—as I learned on my third morning at the Lodge

I was playing chess with my Special, Dan, when our concentration was shattered by a piercing female scream and a cacophony of male shouts. We shot to our feet, upsetting the board and sending chess pieces clattering around the room. In the hallway, we saw a student nurse crying, and clutching her nursing cap in her hands—her expression a blend of shock and shame. A patient, it turned out, had emerged from his room in the process of masturbating and had ejaculated onto her cap!

The heavy iron door at the end of the hallway swung open, and a short, broad-shouldered young man dressed totally in white rushed into the nursing station, with an unusually-large ring of keys dangling from his belt.

This, I would learn, was Chief Aide Bill Thomas.

In the nursing station, Bill spent about 15 minutes commiserating with the student nurse, gradually lowering her emotional temperature. Then, with the student nurse calmed-down, Bill defused any remaining shock by unlocking the "sharps box," containing razors and other items of potential danger in the hands of patients—removing and brandishing a long knife, asking, "Do *you* want to cut his dick off, or do you want *me* to do it?"

While the others were still laughing, Bill replaced the knife and walked down the hall to the patient who had caused the uproar. "I know you realize that was a very disrespectful thing you did to an innocent person," Bill said, "And come on, I know that's not the way you were brought up."

Bill then escorted the patient to the nursing station, where the patient apologized to the student nurse.

IN MY SECOND WEEK, I began seeing Dr. Sokoloff in her office in the white frame building that looked like a former barn. I worried that she was too "weak" to afford any significant help. I became frustrated by her lack of firm guidance, and what seemed to me her stubborn and narrow concern with what was happening in our relationship.

I noticed that she wore no wedding ring, and asked if she was married. She told me that she was divorced, and living with her children. That, too, made me uneasy: If she had screwed up her own life, how could she help me straighten out mine?

She commented that I tended to intellectualize whatever we happened to be talking about, and she wondered whether that might be a device to avoid examining my feelings. Annoyed, I told her that even if she was right, what was the sense of talking about it? "It's like telling Bonnie she shouldn't drink. She knows that but can't help it." The doctor replied: "I'm not saying stop doing it. I'm just saying it's something we ought to look at."

I didn't get it. I wanted her to teach me how to straighten out my life, and she didn't seem interested. She seemed to agree that my life was on the wrong track, but didn't want to talk about what track I should be on.

She seemed particularly interested in what went on between Morey and me—a matter that would become an increasingly-common focus of our sessions.

XIII

"Insanity Runs In Our Family—It Practically Gallops"

LOOKING BACK AFTER MY first few weeks at the Lodge, I realized that I hadn't seriously considered suicide since that dinner at Normandie Farm on my first night. For sure, the bedlam quality of the Third Floor triggered some wild fears. But not even the whacko antics of Henry and the Mafia Man had undone the uplifting effect of having my personal wants taken seriously.

For as long as I could remember, I had lived in dread of insanity, driven to behave in ways that would convince others of my stability and capability. While part of me assumed I was crazy, another part operated on the principle that "I am what others think I am." Now, formally certified as loony, I *knew* what others thought I was, and I couldn't deny that they were right.

Paradoxically, this was something of a liberating force. My worst fears realized, I felt I had nothing more to lose and nothing to hide. I could be myself—a mental patient—and still engage with others in meaningful ways. Life on a locked ward (at least, on this particular locked ward) was a far cry from the living hell of my lifelong terrorizing fantasies.

Indeed, it ultimately became not just tolerable, but downright enjoyable.

In retrospect, I think my turnaround began almost from the moment of my arrival, kick-started by the intended message, "things are going to be different here"—which came through loud and clear. In sharp contrast to Pinel, my personal wants and needs now clearly carried significant weight.

Clearly, too, did the needs and wants of virtually all patients, no matter how sick or out-of-touch. I began to realize that many of the aides were genuinely fond of the patients whom I merely saw as frightening stereotypes of classic crazy-house images. I had never heard of Frieda Fromm-Reichmann, but her maxim of dealing personally with patients at their own level (and in any way available) had clearly taken hold.

I learned that the aides' indoctrination by Bill Thomas imparted Frieda's philosophy in rather dramatic fashion, via Bill's personal story about his own psychosis and confinement in a Bellevue seclusion room. One morning, after more than a month of isolation and restraint, he greeted a new doctor by holding out his own feces. The doctor accepted the improbable gift, taking it in his hand—a gesture that triggered the beginning of Bill's recovery. Just two weeks later, Bill was working as a restaurant cashier in Times Square. Bill's point, of course, was pure "Frieda-ism": patients *could* get well, but staffers needed to deal with them on whatever level they happened to be functioning.

Social worker Pat Rendahl came to the Lodge about three months after my arrival, and said that she was immediately amazed as to "how free and spontaneous both staff and patients were with each other." She was also impressed by the way she was introduced to each patient: "Mrs. Rendahl, this is Mr. So-and-so"—granting the patients a kind of respect she had never seen at other hospitals.

The dress code (if it merited such a label) added to the "we're-in-this-together" ambience. One aide told me that, on arrival, he was initially "puzzled" by his difficulty in distinguishing staff from patients.

Patients did in fact have a certain amount of input into the daily operation of the hospital. By the second week, for example, as one of the

Main Building's few non-psychotic patients, I was invited to join the patient council and immediately named council secretary. With my fellow crazies, and an ever present guard at my side, I helped draw up a set of grievances to present to our keepers: the most salient being a request for a more-lenient liquor policy related to the weekly Friday afternoon patient cocktail parties held at the Hilltop residence.

The rules were unduly strict, we argued—penalizing patients who have no drinking problem in an effort to protect against abuse by those who do. I had of course never attended one of the cocktail parties, and found it difficult to follow the details of the often-heated discussion. But my confusion didn't prevent me from voting with the majority, and affixing my signature as secretary to the minutes of the meeting which contained our "demands." (Six weeks later, when I would transfer to Hilltop, I would realize that the liquor rules had in fact been relaxed.)

The staff sometimes actively solicited patients' views with regard to administrative decisions, which on one occasion (prior to my arrival) produced one of Dr. Gibson's favorite stories: The staff were considering construction of a new building, and were divided in their opinions about a design featuring a square structure with all-glass inner walls facing onto a center court. Those in favor argued that the ability to see the activity in the court might encourage otherwise passive patients to join in, and they circulated a questionnaire to get patient reaction. The response of Mitzi, the Fourth Floor bra-flusher, encapsulated in memorable fashion the view that finally prevailed. Across the top of her otherwise-blank questionnaire, she had scrawled the thought, "People with rocks in their heads shouldn't live in glass houses."

Monthly all-hospital meetings gave patients free rein to speak their minds about any issues of their choosing. While this could (and often did) lead to meaningless digression, it sometimes produced positive results. On one occasion, for example, patient pressure at these meetings led to the hospital's purchase of a new, roomier, vehicle for patient excursions.

A patient publication, *The Broadcaster,* reported various items of all-hospital interest, such as staff hiring and departures, Patient Committee reports, and social doings. One item a few months after my arrival, for example, announced that "The Center will be converted into a Left Bank Parisian Café for Saturday evening's dance," featuring a jazz combo organized by a piano-playing aide; wine punch served at a gaudy umbrella-covered bar; and student nurses in French costumes serving as waitresses.

AFTER TWO WEEKS, my "Specials" were discontinued, and a few days later I was given "unaccompanied grounds privileges," allowing me to be off the ward whenever I wished—so long as I stayed within the hospital boundaries and returned by 10 p.m. The same week, Dr. Gibson removed my casts, and I regained full use of my arms.

The Center now became my primary focus of activity. I spent considerable time there, playing chess, bridge, Scrabble, and ping-pong, sometimes with recreational therapist Judy Richardson, but increasingly with patients from the "open" wards. I even discovered that, casts removed, I could play the Center piano—with growing pleasure, as my hands and fingers regained their flexibility. (My talent in this regard, though, was vastly overshadowed by that of another patient who in a few years would become one of the most popular professional musicians in the Washington, D.C. area.)

The other recreational therapist, June Mazer, told me she was casting a patient production of the play *Arsenic and Old Lace,* and suggested that I try out for the male lead role of Archie. I hesitated, because I had never done any formal acting and wondered whether I was even capable at this point of memorizing lines. But I was charmed by June, a tiny, intense, brown-haired young woman—and I was delighted by her sense of irony in choosing such an exquisitely-appropriate production, with a plot featuring two dotty old maids and their wildly-hallucinating nephew.

She gave me a script, and I soon discovered that I *was* capable of remembering lines (which, in itself, provided a morale boost). I briefly recited for

June, and she awarded me the part—not a big surprise, since the competition, if any, was necessarily something less than formidable.

The ensuing weeks of play practice occupied much of my time, and I realized it was more than a means of diversion to pass the time. I was actually enjoying it! The two old maids were played by patients who were quite skilled—one was a professional actress whom I would later watch perform at Washington's Arena Stage—and they provided me with some enormously-welcome tutoring.

In any event, for the final performance, one of my lines—"Insanity runs in our family; it practically gallops"—required no talent whatsoever to draw roars of appreciative laughter from an audience predominantly filled with patients.

XIV
"I Should Have Been Stronger"

MOREY AND HAZEL DROVE down from New York, ostensibly to watch my performance in *Arsenic and Old Lace*. But plainly more important to him was a meeting he had set up for us with an investment colleague in Washington—part of his ongoing campaign to induce me to join him in his own investment operation. While he continued to berate me to Hazel for having deserted the family business, it was clear that his real concern was that, as he experienced it, I had deserted *him*. And until some years later, I unfortunately failed to make clear that my joining him was simply not to be.

Ironically, Morey had himself been castigated by our father for leaving the family business, when he moved to New York to complete *Bridey* and pursue his interest in securities investment. After Morey's death in 1999, as I was cleaning out his files, I came across a copy of a letter he had written to Dad in June of 1954, when he was back in Pueblo for a visit. It dealt with Dad's disappointment over Morey's moving away, and read as follows:

Dear Dad,

   All week I had been trying to decide what kind of present to send you for Father's Day. And then last night something happened to end my dilemma: I saw something take place, a simple little scene involving a father and his son. At that moment I knew that I must, on this day, send something more than a bauble or trinket. Something more than a material gift.

What I saw was my brother-in-law Eddie with his 75-year-old father. Eddie was about to leave on a short trip, so he and his father were saying good-bye. Suddenly the old man threw his arms around his armless son, and he burst into tears. Eddie cried too.

I was baffled. Why the tears and the emotion when the kid was just taking a short trip? Then in a flash I saw the whole story: It wasn't merely a matter of going on a trip—these two had found a moment to say something that they couldn't possibly express in words. They are so full of feeling for each other that it spilled over a little when they said good-bye.

These two have practically nothing in the world. One is very old and almost deaf. And the young fellow is already tired; his back is crooked, and he doesn't even have a pair of arms. They have nothing—nothing, that is, except for this wonderful feeling for each other.

Naturally, I couldn't help thinking about another father-and-son. This other father and son have almost everything—everything except understanding for each other.

And yet there is a striking parallel between these two sets of fathers and sons. Both fathers were subject to bitter disappointment. In Eddie's case, his father was waiting, proudly and jubilantly, for the birth of his baby. He hoped it would be a son. Can you possibly imagine the father's crushing disappointment when he was told that, yes, a son had been delivered—but the son didn't have any arms?

As to the other father, you already know about his disappointment.

In either case, the disappointments were not easy hurdles for the fathers. Still, in both instances, time will likely prove that these things had to be. There is a Bigger Manager out there who works out these plans. Already, for instance, the resentment in the first case has been replaced by an understanding that is beautiful to behold.

And so it will someday be, Dad, for you and me.

Why not, then, let this Father's Day be for us a sort of Father-and-Son Day—when the two of us can sit back silently and see the picture as it is going to be, not so far in the future, after time has already exposed the apparent disappointment as only one more step in a bigger plan?

I can already see that picture. It's a dandy. I hope you can see it, too.

—Morey

I WAS PUZZLED. Was Morey yearning for the kind of warm, intensely personal emotional bond he perceived between Eddie and his father? Or was he simply predicting that what he was doing in New York would prove so successful that Dad would change his mind about the wisdom of Morey's decision to leave the business—when the "apparent disappointment" would be seen "as only one more step in a bigger plan"?

I fear the latter interpretation is the correct one. Morey's book was about to be published, and he had discovered what would be (for him) the highly-lucrative Graham investment strategy. The manner in which Morey lived the last 45 years of his life would indicate that he probably had no concept of the kind of emotional connection reflected in that Eddie-and-father hug. Rather, what he wanted from others—*needed*, in a most basic sense—was respect, adoration, and a kind of Pavlovian submission to his control.

While Morey and I were both, in a sense, victims of our parents' mismatch, I suspect that he suffered more than I from their unhappy marriage.

Our parents had dated only once before Dad proposed—via a letter mailed from Pueblo to her home in Denver. Mother at first said no, but her father convinced her to change her response because he thought that, as a businessman, Dad could provide well for her. A love tryst, it was not. And as I would learn from Dad's sister, my Aunt Rose, Mother was appalled when she became pregnant almost immediately after the wedding.

Morey was, quite literally, an unwanted child. To Mother, he was the nail in a marital coffin. And while Dad might have envisioned Morey as a likely future business partner, he took basically no interest in Morey's growing-up years.

So Morey found his life interests elsewhere, aided by his superior intelligence, attractive appearance, and physical capability. He made many friends, some of whom he went out of his way to help—such as his friend Herb Elliot. Typically, however, as with Herb, these relationships were of the mentor-mentee variety, with Morey as the tutor. As an all-A student popular with the girls, Morey had a number of Herb-style friendships in which he maintained a high degree of control over the others.

Sadly, however, there is no convincing evidence that Morey was capable of experiencing the kind of emotional bond that existed between Eddie and his father. His relationship with his wife underscored the tragically self-defeating nature of his aspiration to a kind of absolute dominion over his personal world.

Morey and Hazel were divorced, at Hazel's instigation, seven years after the publication of *Bridey*. When her lawyer asked her to list examples of Morey's behavior warranting a divorce, she responded with some 60 single-spaced typewritten pages of his misdoings. After Morey's death, she mailed me a copy of those 60 pages, with a cover note that read:

"This is the first time for a few years that I have read this. I can't help but be appalled at some of it. You would think there were never any good times. There were, but not enough to offset the bad... I should have been stronger. Perhaps I could have helped Morey."

At first, I scoffed at the notion that Hazel's behavior was in any way responsible for their marital misfit. As the Chestnut Lodge social worker had noted, Hazel's desire to help others amounted to a *need*—she was virtually addicted to giving to others. But, on further thought, I realized that her very predilection (however saint-like), could in this instance have been an important element in their ultimate marital failure. She had no bent for criticism or confrontation, and she arranged her days in total keeping with Morey's whims and desires. By so doing, as I see it now, she pampered and nourished his passion for control.

Ironically, when she *did* press one of her own desires, shortly after they were married, the outcome was not only perverse, but would come to haunt her down through the years.

I played a role in what turned out to be a long-term fiasco, to wit:

HAZEL VERY MUCH wanted to have children and was told by her doctor that there was no reason she couldn't become pregnant. When after some months she nevertheless failed to do so, they consulted a doctor in Denver who told Morey, "Mr. Bernstein, you have plenty of spermatozoa, but they are all dead."

So Morey and Hazel asked me to be the donor in an artificial insemination attempt, and however skittish I may have been at the prospect of producing my contribution in a doctor's office, I agreed. The three of us drove to the Colorado Springs office of an internist who was a high school classmate of Morey's.

There, to make certain that Morey's sperm was the problem, the doctor had Morey and Hazel adjourn to a private room where Morey produced a sample. Then, lo and behold, we were all treated to a microscopic view of thousands of very active sperm. I was relieved—but Hazel, of course, was concerned about the accuracy of her own doctor's assurance of her fertility.

As it turned out, her doctor was simply wrong. Further examination revealed that she was in fact incapable of becoming pregnant, and she had to accept the disheartening fact that she would never give birth.

That Colorado Springs incident, moreover, would bedevil her in other ways for the remainder of their marriage. For Morey never lost his love of recounting the event in social gatherings.

"To Morey, it was all a joke, and made for good conversation," Hazel told me. "Not to matter that it was very embarrassing to me—or to other people. He had no sensitivity about it, and he would make a big deal about it and embellish it to suit his fancy.

"Whether in a small group of people, or at a cocktail party where there were many people present, somehow he would inject this story into the conversation. I had begged him not to tell it. I thought it crude, in poor taste, besides being embarrassing to me."

Hazel was embarrassed also by Morey's frequent use of the "F" word. She was pleased when a friend objected to it one night at a social gathering. Morey replied that he was surprised anyone should be offended, but that he would stop using it. Then, however, according to Hazel, "he went into a long dissertation about the kind of people who objected to the use of four-letter words—that in a way, it was even more objectionable than the four-letter words themselves, because he made it sound as though anyone who objected was a fool of some kind."

It is entirely possible, of course, that Hazel, wholly disillusioned, might have exaggerated her descriptions of Morey's behavior. But her comments nevertheless leave little doubt that it was not emotional bonding, but dominion over his personal world, that rated as Morey's top priority.

XV

"I Decided To Take a Chance"

For morey, given his nature, the Lodge staff's refusal to bow to his every whim was a major frustration. For me, in retrospect, it was a liberating force. I now had a new guru in Dr. Gibson, whose aim was to *liberate* me from the tie of servility.

When Dr. Gibson recommended that I move from his maximum security ward to Hilltop, I was reluctant to do so. Life on a locked ward—where I was personally free to come and go as I pleased, some 14 hours a day—had become quite pleasant, and I had to be practically evicted by Dr. Gibson.

Once there, though, I liked living at Hilltop. In what resembled a pleasant country inn, I shared an often-sunlit bedroom with a friendly-but-taciturn middle-aged internist who was there in an attempt to deal with an alcoholic bent.

Hilltop was formally designated a "semi-open" residence, and its patients were on varying degrees of restriction. But its front door was never locked, and like several other patients, I had unlimited privileges on the property.

I quickly discovered Dietle's Tavern in downtown Rockville, a large indoor beer garden populated each night by Lodge aides, outpatients, and occasionally student nurses. Hard liquor and wine were not available—by county law, these were served only at four favored restaurants elsewhere in the county—so occasions of actual drunkenness were rare. But the atmosphere was convivial, and there I became closer with (among others) the aide Brian and the student nurse Pat Brown.

Twice, in defiance of all sorts of Lodge rules, I rode with Pat in the back seat of Brian's car to a secluded spot where she and I smooched, while Brian and a friend of Pat's did the same in the front seat.

Days after that second tryst, the students completed their training stint and returned to North Carolina, replaced by a new contingent from the same nursing school. Dr. Sokoloff's records noted that Pat's departure so saddened me that I sobbed in my ensuing session with her.

Looking back, the improvement in my relations with Dr. Sokoloff is revealed by the very fact that I was willing to tell her about my goings-on with Pat Brown: apparently, I trusted her not to disclose this breach of Lodge rules to the administrators—and she never did. My confidence in her had grown (however slowly) as I gradually became aware that her reserved, understated exterior masked a formidable will.

Early on we clashed regularly, sometimes owing to my spells of spoiled-child willfulness. Once, for example, without consulting her, I talked another of her patients into trading appointments with me, so that I wouldn't have to interrupt a game of bridge I was involved in at the Center. When I did see her, she was quite angry that I hadn't first consulted her about the matter, and her notes recorded that at one point I had shouted, "I fail to see that the switch was any skin off your butt."

In general, though, we gradually became partners in a joint exploration of my befuddled soul. I came to realize that Dr. Sokoloff's function wasn't to teach me how to live my life, but to help me understand who I was and why I behaved as I did.

Thus, for example, we talked about my mother's apparent conviction that I was "sickly" and "not as strong as the other boys." In Dr. Sokoloff's words at a staff conference, "only by being sick" could I have a relationship with my mother "that was at all satisfying." I came to realize that despite my interest in sports and other physical activities, I had to a meaningful extent accepted that alleged "sickliness" as a given. We talked about how Morey had taken over as my father figure—and how now, as he and Hazel visited frequently from New York, he continued to urge me to join him in his investment operation in New York.

I gradually found it easier to talk about my social encounters, my fears and anxieties, my dreams, and occasionally (but at first quite tentatively) about what I might want for myself in the future.

I told her I didn't think her psychiatric training had anything to do with why she was helping me—that it was simply because she was acting in effect as a good friend. She disagreed, pulling down a Freudian textbook to point out some psychiatric concepts she found useful. But she could hardly deny the crucial importance of doctor-patient rapport, the crux of the "Dr. Frieda" concept.

INCREASINGLY, I WAS spending my time in Rockville with various out-patients living in apartments there—including Rocky and Janice, who hailed from two of the wealthiest families in America, and who lived in separate units in the same apartment house. (Rocky's family owned one of the country's largest chains of newspapers, and Janice's family had been a pillar of Philadelphia society since colonial times.) Rocky and Janice spent much of their time playing bridge, and I frequently joined in. When I did, the fourth hand was often played by Ellen, a divorced woman who was the manager of their apartment house.

Soon, I was feeling so good that, despite the pleasantness of Hilltop, I felt ready to become an outpatient. I had spent so much time in downtown Rockville, then only some four square blocks in size, that I already felt like a local resident—moving into an apartment seemed like a quite natural thing to do. With the accord of Dr. Sokoloff and the Lodge medical director, I rented a one-bedroom apartment a few blocks away from the one managed by Ellen, and bought a few items of cheap furniture to make it minimally livable.

Morey and Hazel, who had driven my car cross-country from Palo Alto to New York after leaving me at Pinel, now left the car with me in Rockville. Having been committed to the hospital under Maryland law, I had to qualify for my driver's license by passing all the tests, both written and behind-the-wheel, required of first-time applicants.

I was ready (at least theoretically) to begin my life anew.

A few days before I moved out of Hilltop, as I was packing some clothes to move to my apartment, the charge nurse knocked at my door and entered with a young couple who looked to be in their mid-twenties. The man was being admitted as a patient, I was told, and would room with me until I moved out. They were introduced as Ted and Phyllis. We chatted for a few moments, and I left for my apartment.

The following day, I was told that Ted had been transferred to the Main Building's Third Floor after attempting suicide by starting a car in the parking lot and lying down behind it with his head near the exhaust pipe. It was the last I ever saw of Ted—but his wife Phyllis would become a lifelong friend.

Some years later, Phyllis Reynolds Naylor would publish a book, *Crazy Love,* about her marriage to Ted and how his schizophrenia had doomed their marriage. In it, she would write that Hilltop "looked like a retreat for artists and writers—clean, attractive, like someone's country home. People moved in and out the door with tennis rackets or sat in the big living room reading and listening to music." Ted's roommate, she wrote, "was being discharged in a week." She identified the roommate as "Bill Goldberg" and wrote: "If, when Bill came here, he was as sick as Ted, then this was indeed a place of miracles."

Unfortunately, the Lodge's miracle-working would not extend to Ted.

It would take me several weeks, during which I continued to spend some time each day on the Lodge grounds, to become comfortable living on my own. But I pushed myself to enroll in a drama course at Catholic University in Washington a half-hour drive away, and (encouraged by the Lodge drama coach, June Mazer) joined the Rockville Little Theater group.

June and I had become quite friendly, but when I asked her for a date, she turned me down, citing the formal Lodge prohibition. I thought she was being unduly heedful of a rule that, as I had learned, was routinely ignored. It was only some years later that I learned a more important reason for her reluctance to date me, when I stumbled across a reference to her lasting legacy: The June L. Mazer Lesbian Archive at UCLA.

All my life, I had lived in dread of others learning of my inner woes. Now, it was virtually impossible to hide from those I met in Rockville the fact that I was a Lodge outpatient. Somewhat shockingly, I realized not only that I now really didn't care, but that neither did most of the residents of a town accustomed to dealing with outpatients, and who were grateful to an institution important to its economic base.

To my delight, I must admit, these circumstances led to one of the most active romantic periods of my life. Among others, I dated my bridge partner, the apartment house manager Ellen; a Hilltop nurse, Jean (with whom I had become friendly while living there); and Laura, the 20-year-old cutie who alternated between in- and outpatient status as she fought her alcohol and drug addictions.

More importantly, my life took a major turn when Ellen told me that she knew the editor of the local weekly newspaper and that he was looking for a reporter. His name, she said, was Roger Farquhar, and the newspaper office was two blocks away, on Rockville's main street, Montgomery Ave.

I called Farquhar, and he told me to come right over. With my knees shaking only slightly, I entered the office of the editor of *The Montgomery County Sentinel*.

"I'm told you think you're a reporter," Farquhar said with a friendly smile. He appeared to be in his early 40s, and I would learn that for many years he had been a reporter and editor with the *Washington Post*.

"Well, I have had some experience as one," I ventured timidly. I explained the kind of work I had done with the Palo Alto paper, and he gave me an assignment to cover the next county school board meeting two nights hence.

"I was hesitant about hiring a mental patient," Roger would later tell me. "But I was in desperate need of a good reporter and I decided to take a chance."

So it was that I took over a job that a few years later would be filled by Bob Woodward before he moved on to the *Washington Post* and became a renowned reporter and author of numerous best-selling nonfiction books.

My principal assignment was coverage of the county schools, and when I attended my first school board meeting two nights after meeting Roger, I sat at the press table with two more people who would become lifetime friends. One of them was Phyllis (the wife of my one-day Hilltop roommate Ted) who was now an employee of the Montgomery County Education Association. The other was my predecessor at the *Sentinel*, Dorothy Waleski—who, I learned, had left the weekly to become the head of public relations for the school board.

Phyllis is now the author of some 140 books, and her awards—including the highly prestigious Newbery Medal—are numerous. As I write, she and I are the only surviving members of a close-knit group that we fondly called our Rockville "family," which included Phyllis' second husband Rex Naylor, Roger Farquhar and his wife Mary, Dorothy Waleski and her husband George, the Sentinel photographer Hugh Gillespie, and a young woman I dated for some time during my stay there.

XVI

"See Ya In Brideyville"

THUS DID A LOONY bin change my life inalterably for the better. While I would suffer two later intense depressions, the advent of antidepressant medication ultimately put that devil to rest.

I worked as a reporter and columnist for the Sentinel for about a year and a half, and then decided to go to law school. After graduating first in my law school class, I worked as an appellate lawyer with the Tax Division of the United States Department of Justice, and as a tenured law professor at Southern Methodist University in Dallas, Texas. I have written two books and published essays in, at last count, some 70 newspapers.

Marriage to a fellow DOJ lawyer ultimately ended in divorce, but produced two lovely daughters. One, Sharon, is married, the mother of my two grandsons, and a co-founder and deputy director of Family Forward Oregon, a non-profit organization dedicated to family-supportive legislation. The other, Bobbi, is a multi-award-winning trial lawyer with the U.S. Department of Justice, married to her long-time same-sex partner. (Bobbi's coming-out inspired my first book, *Straight Parents, Gay Children: Keeping Families Together*.)

Myrna and Bob Bernstein

My second marriage, in its 36th year as I write, has been a total blessing. My wife Myrna is highly intelligent, knowledgeable, and talented, with a singularly-caring and compassionate nature. One of her sons by her first marriage, Douglas Nebert, was a world-renowned geologist before his untimely death at age 51 in a plane crash, and an annual award of the U.S. Geological Survey now bears his name. A second son, Dietrich Nebert, is an innovative 5th- and 6th-grade science teacher and founder of the I.S.L.E. Project, which conducts annual Hawaii expeditions for students and their parents.

So my post-loony bin life has been blessed with good fortune. And for that, I remain profoundly indebted to those dedicated fools at Chestnut Lodge.

For morey, by contrast, his later years were strictly downhill, as he became increasingly reclusive—ultimately confining himself to the low-rent one-bedroom apartment in which he would ultimately die of malnutrition.

For a time, he was occupied with dismantling the family business, which included gifting the major part of its property to the City of Pueblo, now occupied by the Pueblo Convention Center. He did, however, retain a small plot with a three-room structure that for some years served as an office for his personal investment activity, where he was assisted by a longtime acquaintance who became a kind of paid attendant-nurse.

It was during this period that, to Myrna and me, Morey's mental state appeared to seriously decline. A prime example is a letter he wrote me in December of 1982 in which, in five long single-spaced typewritten pages, he described quite graphically what a despicable person I was. Among other things, he accused me of constantly "pissing away money," and closed: "But you are not a damn fool. You chose a brother who would work himself to death so that you would never have to give one thought in Hades about your incredible extravagance." And he warned me that another scathing letter would follow: "Chum, Ole Boy, I haven't even started. Perhaps you should buy a suit of armor for your own Christmas gift." (I don't recall any such follow-up letter.)

Still, for most of his life, the element of "goodness" spotted by the Chestnut Lodge social worker was evident throughout Morey's life, displayed most clearly by his ever readiness to drop whatever he might be doing to come to the aid of others in need. I can't count the number of times he did so for me—such as in 1958 when I expressed my panic and he immediately flew to Palo Alto and then with me to Seattle so I could be admitted to Pinel Hospital. He was similarly attentive to our parents and to our Uncle Abe up to their deaths, especially in Abe's last years after he suffered a debilitating heart attack.

By his late 60s, however, Morey had given up even driving his car, and he rarely left his apartment. One exception occurred one night every few weeks when his attendant would drive him to a barber shop whose owner was willing to accommodate Morey's need to have his hair cut in private.

Ultimately, he stopped leaving his apartment altogether, and refused to see anyone other than the attendant. Myrna and I did manage on a few occasions to persuade the attendant to allow us in, and even managed for a time to hire a practical nurse to tend to Morey and the apartment twice a week. But he ended that arrangement after just a few weeks and continued his descent into torpor. The last time we saw him, a few months before his death, he was painfully emaciated; his scraggly, unkempt hair and eight-inch beard spotted with dried Ensure; his pajama top likewise coated with Ensure; his fingernails long and dirty. A gallon jug, apparently a makeshift urinal, sat in an adjacent wastebasket.

Ultimately, Morey's death certificate would officially list his cause of death as "malnutrition." A week after his death, I conducted a memorial service in—where else?—the Bernstein Brothers Room of the Pueblo Convention Center, attended by a dozen or so surviving friends and a number of former employees, in addition to his relatives.

"So long, Chum," was my closing line. "See ya in Brideyville."

NOTE

FOR THOSE WHO ARE interested in Bob's life story, and/or the Bridey Murphy phenomenon, there is a Facebook page (facebook.com/TheSheikandtheShadow), as well as a website (thesheikandtheshadow.com). Also, Bret Bezona of Pueblo, Colorado has an extensive collection of memorabilia, as does the Pueblo County Historical Society, and there are displays about Bridey Murphy and the Bernstein family business at the Pueblo Convention Center.